RACIAL CATEGORIZATION OF MULTIRACIAL CHILDREN IN SCHOOLS

Critical Studies in Education and Culture Series

Racial Categorization of Multiracial Children in Schools

Jane Ayers Chiong

Critical Studies in Education and Culture Series
Edited by Henry A. Giroux

BERGIN & GARVEY
Westport, Connecticut • London

Library of Congress Cataloging-in-Publication Data

Chiong, Jane Ayers, 1948– .
    Racial categorization of multiracial children in schools /
Jane Ayers Chiong.
        p. cm.—(Critical studies in education and culture series,
    ISSN 1064–8615)
        Includes bibliographical references (p.) and index.
        ISBN 0–89789–499–5 (alk. paper)
        1. Racially mixed people—Education—United States. 2. Children
    of interracial marriage—United States—Race identity.
    3. Categorization (Psychology) 4. Identity (Psychology)—United
    States. I. Series.
    LC3621.C53   1998
    371.829—dc21   97–40998

British Library Cataloguing in Publication Data is available.

Library of Congress Catalog Card Number: 97–40998

ISBN: 0–89789–499–5
ISSN: 1064–8615

First published in 1998

Bergin & Garvey, 88 Post Road West, Westport, CT 06881
An imprint of Greenwood Publishing Group, Inc.

Printed in the United States of America

The paper used in this book complies with the
Permanent Paper Standard issued by the National
Information Standards Organization (Z39.48–1984).

10 9 8 7 6 5 4 3 2 1

*This book is dedicated
in memory of my mother and father,
Walter and Mary Boland Ayers*

Contents

Series Foreword

Educational reform has fallen upon hard times. The traditional assumption that schooling is fundamentally tied to the imperatives of citizenship designed to educate students to exercise civic leadership and public service has been eroded. The schools are now the key institution for producing professional, technically trained, credentialized workers for whom the demands of citizenship are subordinated to the vicissitudes of the marketplace and the commercial public sphere. Given the current corporate and right wing assault on public and higher education, coupled with the emergence of a moral and political climate that has shifted to a new Social Darwinism, the issues which framed the democratic meaning, purpose, and use to which education might aspire have been displaced by more vocational and narrowly ideological considerations.

The war waged against the possibilities of an education wedded to the precepts of a real democracy is not merely ideological. Against the backdrop of reduced funding for public schooling, the call for privatization, vouchers, cultural uniformity, and choice, there are the often ignored larger social realities of material power and oppression. On the national level, there has been a vast resurgence of racism. This is evident in the passing of anti-immigration laws such as Proposition 187 in California, the dismantling of the welfare state, the demonization of black youth that is taking place in the popular media, and the remarkable attention provided by the media to forms of race talk that argue for the intellectual inferiority of blacks or dismiss calls for racial justice as simply a holdover from the "morally bankrupt" legacy of the 1960s.

Poverty is on the rise among children in the United States, with 20 percent of all children under the age of eighteen living below the poverty line. Unemployment is growing at an alarming rate for poor youth of color, especially in the urban centers. While black youth are policed and disciplined in and out of the nation's schools, conservative and liberal educators define education through the ethically limp discourses of privatization, national standards, and global competitiveness.

Many writers in the critical education tradition have attempted to challenge the right wing fundamentalism behind educational and social reform in both the United States and abroad while simultaneously providing ethical signposts for a public discourse about education and democracy that is both prophetic and transformative. Eschewing traditional categories, a diverse number of critical theorists and educators have successfully exposed the political and ethical implications of the cynicism and despair that has become endemic to the discourse of schooling and civic life. In its place, such educators strive to provide a language of hope that inextricably links the struggle over schooling to understanding and transforming our present social and cultural dangers.

At the risk of overgeneralizing, both cultural studies theorists and critical educators have emphasized the importance of understanding theory as the grounded basis for "intervening into contexts and power . . . in order to enable people to act more strategically in ways that may change their context for the better."[1] Moreover, theorists in both fields have argued for the primacy of the political by calling for and struggling to produce critical public spaces, regardless of how fleeting they may be, in which "popular cultural resistance is explored as a form of political resistance."[2] Such writers have analyzed the challenges that teachers will have to face in redefining a new mission for education, one that is linked to honoring the experiences, concerns, and diverse histories and languages that give expression to the multiple narratives that engage and challenge the legacy of democracy.

Equally significant is the insight of recent critical educational work that connects the politics of difference with concrete strategies for addressing the crucial relationships between schooling and the economy, and citizenship and the politics of meaning in communities of multicultural, multiracial, and multilingual schools.

Critical Studies in Education and Culture attempts to address and demonstrate how scholars working in the fields of cultural studies and the critical pedagogy might join together in a radical project and practice informed by theoretically rigorous discourses that affirm the critical but refuse the cynical, and establish hope as central to a critical pedagogical and political practice but eschew a romantic utopianism. Central to such a project is the issue of how pedagogy might provide cultural studies theorists and educators with an opportunity to engage pedagogical practices that are not only transdisciplinary, transgressive, and oppositional, but also connected to a wider project designed to further racial, economic, and political democracy.[3] By taking seriously the relations between culture and power, we further the possibilities of resistance, struggle, and change.

Critical Studies in Education and Culture is committed to publishing work that opens a narrative space that affirms the contextual and the specific while simultaneously recognizing the ways in which such spaces are shot through with issues of power. The series attempts to continue an important legacy of theoretical work in cultural studies in which related debates on pedagogy are understood and addressed within the larger context of social responsibility, civic courage, and the reconstruction of democratic public life. We must keep in mind Raymond Williams's insight that the "deepest impulse (informing cultural politics) is the desire to make learning part of the process of social change itself."[4] Education as a cultural pedagogical practice takes place across multiple sites, which include not only schools and universities but also the mass media, popular culture, and other public spheres, and signals how within diverse contexts, education makes us both subjects of and subject to relations of power.

This series challenges the current return to the primacy of market values and simultaneous retreat from politics so evident in the recent work of educational theorists, legislators, and policy analysts. Professional relegitimation in a troubled time seems to be the order of the day as an increasing number of academics both refuse to recognize public and higher education as critical public spheres and offer little or no resistance to the ongoing vocationalization of schooling, the continuing evisceration of the intellectual labor force, and the current assaults on the working poor, the elderly, and women and children.[5]

Emphasizing the centrality of politics, culture, and power, *Critical Studies in Education and Culture* will deal with pedagogical issues that contribute in imaginative and transformative ways to our understanding of how critical knowledge, democratic values, and social practices can provide a basis for teachers, students, and other cultural workers to redefine their role as engaged and public intellectuals. Each volume will attempt to rethink the relationship between language and experience, pedagogy and human agency, and ethics and social responsibility as part of a larger project for engaging and deepening the prospects of democratic schooling in a multiracial and multicultural society. *Critical Studies in Education and Culture* takes on the responsibility of witnessing and addressing the most pressing problems of public schooling and civic life, and engages culture as a crucial site and strategic force for productive social change.

Henry A. Giroux

NOTES

1. Lawrence Grossberg, "Toward a Genealogy of the State of Cultural Studies," in Cary Nelson and Dilip Parameshwar Gaonkar, eds. *Disciplinarity and Dissent in Cultural Studies* (New York: Routledge, 1996), 143.

2. David Bailey and Stuart Hall, "The Vertigo of Displacement," *Ten 8* 2:3 (1992), 19.

3. My notion of transdisciplinary comes from Mas'ud Zavarzadeh and Donald Morton, "Theory, Pedagogy, Politics: The Crisis of the 'Subject' in the Humanities," in *Theory Pedagogy Politics: Texts for Change*, Mas'ud Zavarzadeh and Donald Morton, eds. (Urbana: University of Illinois Press, 1992), 10. At issue here is neither ignoring the boundaries of discipline-based knowledge nor simply fusing different disciplines, but creating theoretical paradigms, questions, and knowledge that cannot be taken up within the policed boundaries of the existing disciplines.

4. Raymond Williams, "Adult Education and Social Change," in *What I Came to Say* (London: Hutchinson-Radus, 1989), 158.

5. The term "professional legitimation" comes from a personal correspondence with Professor Jeff Williams of East Carolina University.

Preface

Imagine a scenario in which a mother takes her first child to kindergarten to register for school. She fills out a registration form whereby she encounters the question, "Please check which one category best represents your child's race." As the mother of a racially mixed child, she does not know which race to choose, so she tells herself, "I'll play it smart either by not checking any or by checking them all."

Racial categorization of children has become increasingly important as a measure to ascertain diverse needs among students as well as the appropriate manner by which teachers and other school personnel might respond to such needs through increased awareness and understanding. The concern that emanates from such awareness and understanding becomes evident through the development of new curricula, cultural enrichment programs, and other policy changes that affect children.

Multiracial children, who are the offspring of multiple racial unions, have unique needs that are not being met because, among other things, they are categorized on the basis of one race only on school forms. This incomplete categorization affects funding for supportive measures that should be available to meet these children's unique needs, especially those needs that relate to racial identity.

The basic question that this book raises is whether or not the needs of interracial children are being met in the schools. In order to critically analyze this question, the schools' racial categorization procedures as predominant cultural forms were investigated by way of its instruments—both on school forms and on government documents. Additionally, I was interested in how such texts might provide a template for affecting both the formal and "hidden" curricula of the schools; that is, how such procedures might play an important role in the total school environment (i.e., teacher and student perceptions, class discussions, school curricula, book selection, cultural programming and clubs, and other artifacts of school culture).

In order to answer these questions, I gathered all the relevant school and federal documents I could find, including the national census and other federal guidelines provided to the schools to assist them in their procedures. I conducted semistructured interviews with teachers, administrators, and other school personnel as key informants. To establish a focus for the direction of my investigation, theories of radical pedagogy were used to critically analyze the role that these cultural forms and significant personnel might play in fostering or obstructing a positive racial identity in interracial children. Also, a theory of classification was utilized to provide a framework to analyze both the nature and language of our racial categorization procedures and instruments such as school forms.

I was concerned that the schools (and the rest of the American public) unknowingly make the normal racial identity development process problematic for at least some of those students who might want to select more than one racial identity. The word "unknowingly" became important to me since I was concerned that such procedures would become so ingrained in our consciousness that we would not know if we were participants in the process of making multiracial children invisible.

Even the mother I mentioned earlier, who decides to "boycott" such procedures by refusing to check one race for her child, was forced "by her own action" to participate in the process of making her child "invisible" in the schools. It will become evident as this investigation unfolds how our schools have become sites for transforming monoracial identities for multiracial children. Their invisibility in the schools' racial categorizations policies mirrors a wider range of their invisibility in school culture.

Racially mixed children need and deserve the wider support of their schools and communities—from textbooks to cultural programs. Before such support can happen, the classification of multiracial children must change. That change, if it is not to be a mere mechanical effort, must take place only after teachers and the larger community become aware of the unique issues currently faced by interracial children and the extent to which the forms used for racial identification compound those issues.

Acknowledgments

I would like to thank all of my advisors at the University of Massachusetts: Jerri Willett for her guidance and direction of my research; George Urch for having faith in me from the beginning; and to my good friend, Joan Ecklein, whose comments and support were offered whenever needed.

I am most grateful to my husband, Winston Chiong, who guided me as a professor and friend. He also cared for our children while I concentrated on this book.

I would greatly like to thank three women who have served me as friends and mentors: Dottie Frauenhaufer, Joan Chaisson, and my aunt, Lori Boland Hunter. Their advice and support have been consistent for years; their belief in me has allowed me to achieve.

I would also like to acknowledge the support of the teachers and administrators who participated in this research. I am especially grateful to the American Association of Multi-Ethnic Americans (AMEA) and to other individuals and groups in the multiracial community whose efforts in creating awareness resulted in policy changes, improved resources, and valuable information.

1

Do the Schools Make Racial Identity Problematic for Multiracial Children?

INTRODUCTION: SETTING THE SCENE FOR CONFUSION AND OPPOSITION

The idea of investigating how our nation's standards for the classification of race affects interracial students through policies mandated in the schools was presented to me by my child's teacher during the 1988–89 school year. The teacher was from the Caribbean where there is no policy of racial categorization. She said she felt uncomfortable about which race to declare for my daughter, who looks Asian like her father. I thought it significant that I had never been asked about her older sister, who looks White.

As a parent, I had already participated in this process over and over again on many school forms, so I had begun to ignore its absurdity. In fact, I had become so accustomed to it that my original questions about these procedures were pushed from my mind:

"Why can't I identify all of their races? And if I do, will they be recorded?"

"If I must declare one race for them, which one do I choose?"

"Do I choose the White race because they are technically mostly White?"

"Do I choose Chinese or Filipino?"

"Do I choose the race that they best resemble?"

"Do I choose the race that would benefit them the most?"

"Do I try to remain loyal to the race that is the perceived 'underdog'?"

"Do I identify all of my children with the same race even though they look different?"

These real-life happenings, checking monoracial boxes for multiracial children, colloquially known as the "check-one-box-only" policy, has become a very tangible symbol of the multiracial individual's lack of inclusion in American society. Forced to acknowledge only part of their racial heritage, they technically do not exist as a distinct group, which in turn affects how the American public perceives them. And how society perceives them appears to be a very powerful influence on how they view themselves racially. They begin to impose this structure upon their personal identity. Thus, the sociopolitical ramifications of how they would be racially categorized in society were overwhelming for a process that was meant to have an explicit basis for race as if there is a direct correlation between their monoracial classification and their multiracial existence.

Not only do we forget how really odd it is, but many still believe that there is such a notion as a "pure" race even though scientists have refuted the principle consistently throughout history. A. I. Gordon quotes a UNESCO (United Nations Educational, Scientific, and Cultural Organization) study conducted in 1952 by many noted geneticists and physical anthropologists that discusses the matter of "pure races":

There is no evidence for the existence of so-called "pure races." Skeleton remains provide the basis of our limited knowledge about earlier races. In regards to race mixture, the evidence points to the fact that human hybridization has been going on for an indefinite but considerable time. Indeed, one of the processes of race formation and race extinction or absorption is by means of hybridization between the races. (1964: 221)

Thus, he concludes, "The implication that there is a 'pure race' in the sense of never having mixed with any other racial group is, on the basis of historical and biological evidence, not accurate" (1964: 220).

With all the evidence and testimony from scientists, why do we ascribe so much warrantableness to our racial divisions? Why were they created? According to Spickard, "The most important thing about the races was the boundaries between them. If races were pure [or had once been] and if one were a member of the race at the top, then it was essential to maintain the boundaries that defined one's superiority, to keep people from the lower categories from slipping surreptitiously upward. Hence, U.S. law took pains to define just who was in which racial category" (see Root 1992: 15).

Racially mixed peoples, never having been recognized, fall between the cracks of categories created by a racially divided society. This lack of distinctiveness in American society is reflected in both our language and a racial categorization system that refuses to recognize racially mixed people in a distinct manner. Even though throughout American history, a multitude of words have been used to describe them (I counted 29 in my last attempt), almost all are used to describe children of only two racial unions. To further confuse the issue, there is very little consensus about their meaning, nor does any nomenclature correspond with any racial classification. Hence, racially mixed children can be described in a multitude of different and confusing ways, most often as comprising only two races and classified on the basis of one.

Contributing to such inconsistencies are regional differences in how we converse about racially mixed people. In the eastern United States the words "interracial/biracial child" have been used mostly to infer children of Black/White parents; whereas the same terminology is more likely used to describe children of Asian/White racial unions on the West Coast. This reflects the larger number of people who claim their heritage from Black/White couples and live on the East Coast, compared with the larger number of Asian/White couples living on the West Coast. I always felt as a parent on the East Coast that I would be viewed with suspicion if I tried to stake a claim in my children's underdog status by referring to them as being either "interracial" or "biracial." Yet, their Filipino cousins in California thought of them as being "interracial," while their Filipino "aunties" referred to them as being "mestizo." Additionally, I am unaware of any instance on either coast in which the term "biracial" is used except to designate someone from a Black/White mixture.

Such a misunderstanding by the American public as to whom should be included in "bi/inter/multi" racial status is reflected in all aspects of public discussion, especially by the media. Whenever I was contacted by reporters or producers over a 15-year period, I was constantly requested to suggest names of parents and children from Black/White racial unions. In fact, though other groupings are now more likely to be included in public debate than ever before, the recognition of their concerns is still greatly diminished.

Thus, children from racial groupings other than Black/White are often regarded as if they were "marginally interracial." On the one hand, we have the enormous sociopolitical polarization between Blacks and Whites, which has created the assumption that the mixed race issue has a much greater impact on their children than on children from any other racial groups. Yet, this issue could have an even greater impact on the offspring of Asian/White parents because their numbers are greater and their issues may be more of an internal nature. "In the 1990 census, in California, nearly one fourth of children with any Asian background were White and Asian" (*Federal Register*, Office of Management and Budget, August 28, 1996: 44686). Yet, parents of Asian/White children are less likely to be consulted on sociopolitical issues.

Until the introduction of the movement for a new "multiracial" category and its subsequent usage, "interracial" was the most commonly accepted terminology to describe all racially mixed children. The prefix "inter," meaning "between" and "among," makes it adequate to use this term to describe children of any and all racial mixtures. However, it now appears that the word "interracial" has been brought to its demise. I also noticed that it was not listed among a glossary of terms in a recent anthology about the multiracial experience (Root 1996).

Even as I write this book, I pause each time for a private battle about what to call "them." The word "interracial" seems so limited and out of date. Yet the term "multiracial," while meant to be more encompassing of anyone who is racially mixed and has become a very strong positive symbol of this group seeking empowerment and celebration of pride in their community, does create an impression that racially mixed children are something "new." They have been around, if not included or even technically visible, since the beginning of time. Most literature written prior to the 1990s clearly uses the term "interracial" as the reference of choice. Also, not all the teachers I interviewed would have been familiar with the new "multiracial" term. Hence, I use both "interracial" and "multiracial" interchangeably in this book.

OVERVIEW OF WHAT WE HAVE BEEN TAUGHT
ABOUT MIXED RACE PEOPLES

When I first attempted research in this area in the early 1990s, the topic of interracial families and individuals had been grossly undeveloped. At that time, I found only 53 books and monographs written worldwide, and only 35 of them concentrated on American relationships. The words "interracial," "racially mixed," or any other potential keyword including "multiracial" used in a children's library search did not yield any information.

The literature that was available was very old and written from a negative perspective, though unsubstantiated. First, the literature abounds in negative motives for interracial marriage, thus setting the stage for creating an image of instability of those who choose to marry across racial lines and become the parents of "unstable" racially mixed children. Several researchers have noted public perceptions about why people marry interracially (Char 1977; Jeter 1982; Porterfield 1978; Brayboy

1966). I have organized these negative stereotypes under the popular themes that appear over and over again:

Motives

Sexual

1. People who marry outside their race are promiscuous;
2. Relationships between Blacks and Whites are only sexual;
3. Such relationships reflect the failure to resolve the Oedipus/Electra complex;
4. They indicate a psycho-sexual attraction with a different race;
5. They result from sexual fantasies that label one group more sexual than another, a desire for the "forbidden fruit";
6. They make use of the unique opportunity that socially opposed interracial sex offers for acting out their hostility toward parents or society.

Status

1. Minorities marry Whites to gain financial and social status;
2. A person due to a mental, physical, or social handicap may feel inferior and thus enter into an interracial marriage after determining that acceptance will be found only outside the culture of birth;
3. White men who marry Black women come from the lower ranks of society and are not educated.

Rebellion

1. Interracial unions represent marriage as an act of aggression toward another race;
2. They indicate a desire for control and revenge;

3. They signify the desire to rebel against parental authority;
4. They indicate the desire to offend on a conscious or unconscious level;
5. They signify an act of mutual rejection;
6. It was the couple's desire for revenge, not love, that brought them together.

Ego

1. They indicate an adventuresome need to be different, which may be amplified into a narcissistic exhibitionism for attention-getting problems;
2. They may represent a need to display idealistic, non-bigoted liberalism;
3. Idealism may be a motive of a "liberal underdog." Identification with the underdog, an inferiority complex, rebellion, and rescue could be the outgrowths of this idealism.

Neurotic

1. An individual may be exhibiting neurotic self-degradation;
2. A sadomasochistic marriage can involve a "slave" who can be controlled, humiliated, hurt, and teased because the partner has alienated family and friends by entering the marriage;
3. A person may marry into the culture of an early caretaker, thus demonstrating a fixation with an early love object;
4. A mixed marriage may signify the desire to punish oneself, "the exquisite torment";
5. The primary difference in interracial situations is that the broader social problems accentuate the neurotic potential.

Race/Gender Specific

1. Asian women who marry White men are lazy, uneducated, do not understand English, and are the "property" rather than wives of their White husbands;
2. Asian females intermarry to escape the "traditional Asian male role";
3. White females and Black males attract one another because both are oppressed by White men;
4. White men who marry Black women come from the lower ranks of society and are not educated;
5. The White female was perceived as a status symbol;
6. The Black or White female was pregnant.

Second, recorded information suggested that interracial couples bring this instability into marriage, where they are also marginalized by society. Popular theories of the "marginal man" viewed racially mixed individuals and families as being unstable because they were excluded from belonging to any one, established group. This caused them to be isolated and outside the mainstream of American public life (Park 1928; Stonequist 1937). Consequently, social scientists who had studied racial intermarriage often examined the same hypotheses about the following negative issues: the stability or instability of such marriages (Connor 1976; De Vos and Wagatsuma 1972; A. I. Gordon 1964), identity confusion in their children (Gibbs 1987; Lyles et al. 1985; Sommers 1964; Teicher 1968), negative motives for marrying (Jeter 1982; Porterfield 1978), social isolation from their families and communities (Spickard 1989), and the history of legal social controls against such unions (A. I. Gordon 1964; Spickard 1989). However, it should be noted that some of these authors have also studied interracial families from positive perspectives.

Such conceptions as neurotic motives, marital instability, and marginality in society infected the minds of the American public, including those who wanted to marry outside their race. This brings to mind some of the fears I felt 25 years ago when

I was the first person in my extended family to marry outside my race, religion, and cultural origin. I had no role models. I did not know any Asians well. But I do remember very strongly the images that surfaced in my mind. I remember my fears about any potentially insincere motives that could be buried in my subconscious and that my children would have mental problems. I especially remember the fears of my parents that society was "not ready for us" and would make life very difficult. In fact, they thought it their duty to warn and advise me against marrying interracially, even though they adored my husband. I remember their conflicts expressed in dialogue, "If you obey us and do not marry him, either one or two things are wrong. You either do not love him enough or we didn't raise you right." We were taught to be frightened.

What the literature lacked was an honest attempt to suggest that multiracial families and individuals were victims of external pressures that might be relieved through social change in the society that is responsible for their existence. Also, the literature lacked an analysis of the identity development process of multiracial children and how they may have resolved these issues within a positive framework. Public perception had steered research to expect certain conclusions—mostly negative—about the stability or instability of racially mixed marriages and individuals. Hence, it was clear that changes must occur about the way in which the American public perceives interracial marriages. As has been adequately reported in the literature, wider community acceptance is a key issue to the well-being of interracial couples and their offspring (Johnson and Nagoshi 1986). Also, research written consistently since the 1980s from a more positive perspective (Hall 1980, 1992; Kich 1982, 1992; Arnold 1984; Brown 1995) needs to be shared with the wider society so that multiracial children can be assisted in their self-empowerment.

As a step toward unifying racially mixed individuals through empowerment, new terms are purposely being created by racially mixed people with other racial minorities. We have seen this many times throughout history, most recently during the civil rights movement when minority groups took control of the racial terminology ascribed to them. For example, Negroes and

Coloreds became Blacks or African Americans, Orientals became Asians, American Indians became Native Americans. Such self-designations rather than other-designations become very strong symbols of their pride, strength, and empowerment through unity. Likewise, the advent of the new "multiracial" terminology to encompass children of all racial mixtures is now being used to signify a movement toward renegotiation in and ultimately control of how the American public perceives them. It has already made a difference. Racially mixed children are now being noticed as if they are something "new" and "different" from ever before.

History of Opposition

Racial intermixture has been in existence even before recorded history; the history of opposition to interracial unions stretches back to biblical times. In Numbers XII, I, of the Old Testament there is a suggestion of the fermentation raised against Moses for his interracial marriage: "And Miriam and Aaron spake against Moses because of the Ethiopian woman he had married." And, in Shakespeare's *Othello*, Iago foreshadows the antagonism of Desdemona's family to her marriage to the Moor, described as "thick lips," when he warns her father: "Even now, now, very now, an old black ram is tupping your white ewe. Arise, Arise!"

That such a state of affairs can still exist in the United States would seem an indictment of a nation that claims to be the bulwark of democracy in the free world. As recently as 1960, 29 states had anti-miscegenation laws, and it was illegal to marry outside one's race until 1967 in some states. Yet, today as we approach the twenty-first century, the fight for the basic human right of self-designation is still denied. Thus, one can surmise that our nation is willing to accept interracial marriage, if and only if, multiracial people become invisible and denigrate their distinct group by joining the race of the minority partner.

But this legal control did not just appear recently. The United States has an entire history of monoraciality. The roots of the modern debate on racial categorization can be seen in the history of the nation predating the Civil War. The notion of racial mixture was first rejected when the increase in the mulatto

population rose sharply in comparison to a dwindling population of slaves who were Black. "The South came to the one-drop
rule essentially because it came to accept slavery as its god"
(Williamson 1984: 75). Thus, the antagonism against the mulatto threat to slavery gave birth to the "one-drop rule" that
still prevails today. In fact, Williamson notes a very interesting
connection of mulatto history to African American history:
Since most Blacks are of mixed ancestry that begins in the co-
lonial period as mulatto history and culture and ends in the
twentieth century as Negro history and culture, he is worth
quoting at length:

> The fact that slavery was getting whiter, that in reality
> many slaves were more white than black, was a fact with
> which the proslavery argument could not cope. Either it
> could ignore the problem, which it did explicitly, or it could
> brusquely dismiss it by applying the one-drop rule to per-
> sons in slavery, which it did implicitly. (1984: 62)

A view of the legal map regarding interracial marriage in this
country illustrates this long and continuous history of prevent-
ing interracial unions:

- 1661 First law to deter arose in Maryland. White woman
  servants and their children by Black men had to serve
  their husband's master and their children would be
  slaves.
- 1705 Massachusetts fined and imposed a period of ser-
  vitude for those entering interracial unions. Clergymen
  were also fined for performing the ceremony.
- 1790 First census to include a racial question. Four categories: Free White Males, Free White Females, All
  Other Free Persons, and Slaves.
- 1872 The California Civil Code stated that all marriages
  of White persons with Negroes, Mongolians, members of
  the Malay race, or mulattos are illegal and void. As a
  consequence, interracial marriages were illegal in California until 1948.

- 1880 Statute enacted in California to prohibit racial intermarriage between Mongolians (known today as Asians) and Caucasians.

- 1955 more than half of the states had anti-miscegenation laws on their books and no court in the land except the California Supreme Court had ever declared such laws unconstitutional.

- 1950 Judge Bazile sentenced Richard Loving and Mildred Jeter Loving to one year in jail. Their crime: Mildred is part Negro and part Indian and Richard is white. "Almighty God," he intoned, "created the races White, Black, Yellow, Malay, and Red, and he placed them on separate continents. The fact that he separated the races shows that he did not intend them to mix" (Hollis 1991).

- 1967 *Loving vs. Virginia*. The case went to the U.S. Supreme Court, where it declared anti-miscegenation laws unconstitutional. Chief Justice Earl Warren stated, "There can be no doubt, that restricting the freedom to marry solely because of racial class violates the central meaning of the equal protection clause of the 14th Amendment." At this time, 16 states still had anti-miscegenation laws.

- 1977 Institution of Statistical Policy Directive 15, established by the U.S. Office of Management and Budget (OMB) (see Appendix B.1). It divided people into four racial categories: American Indian/Alaskan Native, Asian/Pacific Islander, Black, and White and breaks down ethnicity into "Hispanic origin" and "Not of Hispanic origin." This policy validated and re-established the racist rule of hypodescent (one drop only) for racial classification supposedly for the purpose of protecting the rights of minorities following the desegregation movements of the civil rights era. But this policy, a "throw back" to the slave trade and the goal to "keep the races 'pure,' " furthered the segregation, isolation, and invisibility of racially mixed peoples by classifying them erroneously on the basis of one race only. Additionally, "self-identification is not the preferred method among Federal agencies. . . . They prefer to collect racial and ethnic data by visual observation" (OMB Federal Register, August 1995: 44679). According to Carlos Fernandez, who drafted and delivered AMEA's testimony to Congress, this is "the last vestige of segregation in America, which is maintained by current federal regulation" (see Root 1996: 25).

CONCLUSION

Public perception seems to be a key factor in determining the stability or instability of racially mixed marriages and peoples, their marginality or inclusion and their "self" rather than "other" designations. When research literature granted legitimacy to theories of instability, marginality, and otherness, the American public, including interracial families and individuals, framed or shaped the experience of members of this group. When one looks at all the confusion and negative viewpoints, it is no wonder that members of this community would feel some sense of instability, isolation, and identity confusion. They had become until now a people "messed up by their multipleness."

Public perception affects personal perception. How our nation racially classifies people of mixed race shapes such distorted public perception. Individuals of "more than one race" are forced to identify themselves on the basis of "one race only," which is a monoracial limitation of the American language. Therefore, their full racial identities are not expressed—remain technically invisible—and the possibilities for how they are to be viewed are controlled.

The template for deciding these categories is based on Statistical Policy Directive 15, the ultimate authority for racial/ethnic classification on all of our government forms, and thus all forms affecting the public sector. This government mandate licenses our institutions of learning, public health, banking, employment, social security, and even our national census to camouflage their unique needs, thus affecting funding for supportive measures that should be made available to them. These measures include medical screening for organ donation and genetic diseases as well as their inclusion in school books, cultural programming, curricula, and other aspects of school culture that affect racial identity.

Any changes in these procedures and ultimately how the racially mixed child is perceived will result from efforts by members of that child's community. Through their newsletters, conferences, letter writing, and demonstrations, multiracial community groups have been unrelentless in trying to change school policy on how their children are racially categorized and perceived in the schools. Though efforts have been extensive, they have yet to be viewed as a powerful force. Despite the increased multicultural awareness since the mid-1970s, almost never has the multiracial community been included in any distinct way in all aspects of the American public experience.

Multiracial groups and organizations lack the numbers and thus political influence of other established groups. This has resulted in the inability of agencies to gain the support of funding sources. Members of the American Association of Multi-Ethnic Americans (AMEA), an umbrella organization for over 45 other local groups nationwide, have not been successful in attaining funds and so are dependent upon volunteers and donations. When I was the Founder/Director of the Multiracial Family Network (MFN) in Boston, I was not able to gain funds except for very small projects. What is most difficult is approaching funding sources that have supported other established minority groups. One major funding source, though intrigued by the issues presented, wanted me to "keep them in mind for the future." A board member of another foundation that funds grassroots community groups phoned me (which was not official procedure) to express her vehement opposition to interracial marriage. This took place in the early and mid-1980s, a time, I felt, when multiracial families were still not considered to be "politically correct." Thus, though there is great need to create national consciousness about multiracial families, they need the money from charitable organizations and individuals to create consciousness and the consciousness to raise the money.

Finally, the issue of how we categorize mixed race individuals is gaining national attention as we approach our next census in the year 2000. The option of a new multiracial category is currently being debated and members from the multiracial community have been included in the discussions. But there is a lot of opposition from other groups with more political influence.

The movement for a new multiracial category should be upheld if only for the reason that such individuals are claiming their right to do so. Language, as we will see in subsequent chapters, is a powerful influence on public perception. It is not merely a reflection of society's viewpoints; it structures those perceptions. It is through language that people internalize the attributes of the social group and, on this basis, form their own subjective attributes about themselves in their relationships to others. By instilling a new multiracial category, multiracial peoples will intercede with current negative perceptions, shape and compose a new template for positive perceptions, and thus change the very nature of the multiracial experience itself.

2

Mixed Not Messed

No single issue receives more attention in the literature of interracial marriage than the racial and cultural identity of the couples' offspring. Yet until very recently, the information was scarce, highly speculative and nearly always negative. A great deal of the earlier research is based on studies conducted in mental health centers and social service agencies where patients have already been referred for treatment (Gibbs 1987; Sommers 1964; McRoy and Freeman 1986). Based on unrepresentative case histories, the research focused predominantly on children from Black/White unions whom, it is suggested, are more prone toward having identity difficulties than children who are a composite of other racial unions (Gibbs 1987; Sommers 1964; McRoy and Freeman 1986). This work is often biased toward the notion that even if they are not referred for racial identity problems initially, social workers frequently find that such identity problems exist (McRoy and Freeman 1986).

Most of the American public have shaped their notions on Erikson's concept of identity, which he described as "a sense of personal sameness and historical continuity . . . a sense of psychosocial well-being" (1963). He proposed that the central task of adolescence is to form a stable identity and delineated a series of developmental tasks to be negotiated before a positive identity is attained. Successfully passing through these developmental tasks was seen as a personal triumph rather than being imbued with a series of sociopolitical forces that came into play to affect a positive outcome. Racially mixed children, though victims of societal pressures that affect their outcome, have viewed this loss in a very personal way. They were responsible because they failed to successfully cope with their developmental tasks.

However, more recent research has been conducted by authors who are either racially mixed themselves or are involved in interracial relationships and show a sense of commitment and sensitivity to their research. This information is found in recent dissertations, through the newsletters of interracial organizations, and is just beginning to emerge in the publishing world. While not denying that identity problems exist, the focus of this current research is not on whether or not a multiracial child has identity problems but on understanding these issues within a sociopolitical construct and how they were resolved within a positive developmental framework (Kich 1982, 1992; Hall 1980).

In this model, identity formation is conceived not as a result of a private, internal underlining process but "as culturally appropriated modes of discourse by which individuals imbue their actions with rationality and warrantability" (Slugoski and Ginsburg 1989). Identity achievement, rather than being an individual achievement ascribed to intra-psychic processes of which the individual has no control, lies within a more social locus of control, which is not always benign. Taylor is worth quoting at length on this issue: "We define our identity always in dialogue with, sometimes in struggle against, the things our significant others want to see in us . . . thus in discovering my own identity doesn't mean that I work it out in isolation, but that I negotiate it through dialogue, partly overt, partly internal, with others" (1994: 32–33). Thus, failure to or difficulty in achieving a cohesive identity does not constitute a "moral deficit," "lack of control over the process," "lack of ego strength," or "lack of psychosocial effectiveness" (Erikson 1966) but rather "a failure to mesh with society's demands and rewards" (Slugoski and Ginsburg 1989).

Identity formation is a difficult task for all children, especially in a pluralistic society where race is a determining factor. When one is not a member of the majority group, the difficulty deepens and the task is much greater. Hutnik's model (1986) of the strategies that ethnic minority children of one race might adopt suggests the difficulty, although only in part, that interracial children must face. She hypothesized that minority children are forced to adopt one of four strategies for ethnic self-identification.

1. the assimilative strategy: those who see themselves as belonging exclusively to the majority and not to the ethnic minority group.

2. the dissociative strategy: those who see themselves as belonging exclusively to the ethnic minority group and not to the majority group.

3. the acculturative strategy: those who identify with both the minority group and the majority group, and

4. the marginal strategy: those who identify with neither group.

If the process of identity formation is much more problematic for minority children than for white children, then it would be even more difficult for children of a multiracial background. Without community support, all their options must become even more scrambled. While Hutnik's model of the acculturative strategy allows for a multiple identity option that might serve some multiracial children better, the validation of this option is constricted by the rigid monoracial standards of our social order.

How a racially mixed child negotiates his/her racial identity is based on race that is primarily a sociopolitical construct rather than a biological one (Spickard 1989). Racial distinctions were developed initially as a tool of dominance and have been maintained by our inflexible categorization procedures. Our nation's "check-one-box-only" policy is an instrument of our racial social order that legitimizes and enforces our "one-drop rule" not only to make sure that no one who could be identified as Black could also be identified as White; but unfortunately this rule has also been utilized by minority groups to resist White dominance and to show unity and power among their groups. According to Spickard, "Race, this socially constructed identity, can be a powerful tool, either for oppression or for group self-actualization" (1989: 19). Multiracial children represent an upset of this social locus of control. Their increasing existence and visibility are raising issues about previously sanctioned and relatively unchallenged ideas that are at the core of how the American public thinks about race.

It has not been disputed that some interracial children have identity ambivalence that needs to be resolved. However, beginning in the late 1970s a noteworthy shift occurred in the focus of this identity dilemma. Current research is investigating how this "challenge" rather than "crisis" is worked out in a positive manner. The following studies demonstrate the variety of ways in which multiracial individuals incorporated their multiple heritages into their lives:

Hall (1980) interviewed 30 Black/Japanese in the Los Angeles area and found that both those that indicated a Black identity, the majority (18), were as well adjusted as those who indicated a Black/Japanese identity. One indicated a Japanese identity and one refused to categorize himself racially. She sought to measure the extent of their cultural affiliations and found them to be multicultural (harmony between cultures) rather than marginal (conflict between cultures).

Kich (1982, 1992), based on his research with 15 Japanese/White adults in the San Francisco Bay area, developed an interracial identity development model in three stages through which persons come to accept themselves and integrate sometimes disparate parts and experiences into a full sense of self. Using a semi-structured clinical developmental model, he charted the transitory nature of many conflicts throughout childhood and adolescence and into adulthood before a positive resolution was attained, with multiracial individuals having a distinct identity rather than a composite of its parts.

Arnold (1984), in his study of the racial self-concept of 28 Black/White children, found that interracial children do not differ from the norm in self-concept but that they may experience uncertainty about racial issues, for example, ambivalence regarding the race with which to identify. In addition, he found that those children who chose to identify with being interracial had a higher self-concept score. However, it is important to note that Arnold did not find a significant difference between those who do not. Of the 28 children studied, 12 identified themselves as interracial, 11 as black and 5 as white.

Brown (1995) explored the racial self-identification of 119 young adults of mixed Black and White racial heredity. The study failed to verify the common assumption that racial identity formation is a linear journey toward blackness. Most respondents supported an interracial identity and had the least conflict, and for many the Black identity was the publicly expressed identity while the White identity was private. This was viewed as a mechanism in order to cope with societal pressures to negate White roots.

Hence, researchers are still employing the familiar developmental stage model of Erikson. Rather than developing a unique model, some seem to be reincorporating their preconceptions of the stages that racially mixed children must pass through before they go to the next stage on their way to full realization. What concerns me is the ironic similarity to the very concept of fixed, rigid, racial categories (or in this case, stages of development) rather than categories that are more situational, whereby one can move back and forth and overlap in response to individual experiences.

Nonetheless, researchers have shifted to support the viewpoint that interracial children are not necessarily doomed to have a negative self-image, and racially mixed children are

increasingly defying monoracial standards by choosing to identify themselves as "interracial" or "multiracial." Murphy-
Shigematsu (1986) notes an important comparison between one
author's writings in the seventies and eighties. In the seventies
Poussaint (1975) authored an article entitled "The Problems of
Light Skinned Blacks," and several years later he wrote a more
upbeat research report based on his conversations with Harvard students called "Benefits of Being Interracial" (1984).

Regardless, it is clear that there is still reason to be concerned about some of the realities that an interracial child must
face in incorporating a more cohesive identity. Research indicates that the difficulty encountered by the mixed race person
originates externally to the individual in social structures that
idealize racial purity and in which racism is institutionalized.
Reconciling the conflict between what internal experience of
differentness and external attribution of the meaning of this
difference is likely a lifelong developmental process (Bradshaw
1990).

What is most significant is the lack of external support for
interracial families in providing for a healthy self-image of their
children. As long as interracial children live in a society that
still has a singular, fixed notion of identity and that is struggling with its own racial and cultural identity, they will continue to face this issue. Such external pressures exert on the
children and their parents the additional stress of developing
strategies to cope with an unsupportive society. Additionally,
the wider the racial polarization against certain racial groups,
the greater the pressure on the racial identity process for the
individual.

The concept of multiple identity is still too scary an idea and
suggestive of mental disturbance for most of the American public. We have associated the lack of a singular identity with such
negative manifestations as schizophrenia, multiple personality
disorder, or similar negative cues that being "mixed" means
being "messed." The idea that the possession of an array of, or
perhaps even overlapping identity options, is in itself a healthy
choice has not been validated by the American public and expressed in its cultural formations. In fact, attempts by racially
mixed persons to move back and forth between color lines is

viewed suspiciously (e.g., they're "passing as an impostor") rather than as an appropriate strategy in a multiracial world (Bradshaw 1990).

What is most interesting is how much attention is currently and finally given to issues that have been around for a very long time. There is an amazing increase in the literature available in the 1990s. Material is being published at such a fast pace that it is impossible here to record all that is happening. This phenomenon could be a research topic in itself. The answer lies in establishing the complex interconnections between the process the mixed race individual must pass through in order to achieve a cohesive identity and that which our nation is finally confronting through its attempts to renegotiate its concept of race. We are a nation with an identity crisis, and as such we must either incorporate our subcultures into a cohesive whole with flexible borders or remain separate and diverse.

Symbolically, the multiracial individual represents the quest for a new social order predicated on inclusiveness and greater fluidity of social boundaries (Bradshaw, cited in Root 1992: 79). Unless this happens in society, mixed race individuals will continue to be suppressed by a system that legitimizes and transmits their ambivalence.

3

Language: Instruments of Identity

A man who has a language consequently possesses the
world expressed and implied by that language.
                                    —Franz Fanon

How does our society refer to children of mixed racial background? Multiracial children's invisibility in society is reflected
in the language of our racial categorization system that lacks
the distinct words to include them. This lack of a clear difference of identity from monoracial children has been instilled in
our minds and incorporated into our culture in ways that have
defied attempts to change the concept, even though the notion
of a "pure" race has been consistently refuted. Waters is worth
quoting at length about this subject:

The widely held societal definition of race and ethnicity
take the categories and classifications in place at any one
time for granted, and hence do not generally see them as
socially created or dynamic in nature. The common view
among Americans is that ethnicity is primordial, a per-

sonal, inherited characteristic like hair color. . . . In fact, people's belief that racial or ethnic categories are biological, fixed attributes of individuals does have an influence on their identities. (1990: 17, 18)

Such "folk taxonomies" are very real in the minds of the American people.

Since mixed race individuals are "expressed" through the monoracial limitations of our vocabulary, they are in actuality not "expressed" and remain invisible. Add to this the perceived negative impact of what it means to be racially mixed and the stage is set for real harm. Racially mixed people internalize the opinions of others in order to form their own identity. According to Taylor,

Our identity is partly shaped by recognition or its absence, often by the misrecognition of others, and so a person or group can suffer real damage, real distortion, if the people or society around them mirror back to them a confining or demeaning or contemptible picture of themselves. Non-recognition or misrecognition can inflict harm, can be a form of oppression, imprisoning someone in a false, distorted, and reduced mode of being. (1994: 25)

This serves as a constant reminder that they do not fit in or perhaps that they do not exist, a situation that certainly does not support the development of a healthy sense of identity in children.

The "one race only" concept is particularly confusing for a child who possesses the phenotype of one race and the ethnic surname of another, *or* for the child who looks a different race from a sibling, *or* for those who may be raised by a biological, single parent who looks a different race from them, *or* for those who have been singly categorized by others in different races on separate occasions, and so on. Variability in the racial genotype and phenotype of multiracial children is so limitless that they transcend racial stereotypes of how they should look. Yet, they live in a society that transmits very immutable, monoracial messages of how people should look and feel about themselves. Based on these messages, multiracial children reflect on how to formulate their identity.

Thus, how one is racially categorized in society is an important factor for self-identification, because self-image is in part a reflection of what others see in us (Cooley 1964). And when there is a discrepancy between an individual's actual social identity and his/her virtual one, we are likely to give no open recognition to what is discrediting, and the situation can become tense, uncertain, and ambiguous (Goffman 1984).

Regardless of which group a multiracial individual chooses to identify with publicly, it is only normal that there might be a conflict with how that person identifies privately. An environment that offers no positive, viable options to identify monoracially makes it almost impossible for racially mixed individuals to accept and assert a multiracial identity. "The idea that ethnic self-identification is not biological or primordial and that it involves a great deal of choice may be startling to some people, because it is counterintuitive when viewed from the popular conception of ethnicity" (Waters 1990: 16–17). Consequently, there has been little development of a group consciousness among multiracial people (Nakashima 1992: 177).

Also, there is a degree of dissent within the multiracial population, regarding multiracial self-identification for children of Black/White unions who are more racially polarized by society. Those who oppose do so for a variety of reasons. Some are against categorization as a manifestation of White supremacist control and claim that multiracial recognition is an effort of the White establishment to further divide the Black race. Still others feel that society will always see them as Black and so they should be taught to identify as Black. The most powerful concern comes from leaders of the minority population who fear their communities will lose entitlements due to decreased numbers drawn by multiracial members. Hence, it is most important to acknowledge the fact that there are many more external cues and pressures to support the option of choosing to identify with only one race making it a likely "choice" for children from this group.

Some parents accept that people will always need to categorize, that it does exist and that perhaps separate categories are better than none at all, whereby interracial children are invisible. Wardle, a parent of biracial children and researcher on the subject, noted one example of an important consequence that the lack of a separate category can have. "In all areas of success (gifted programs, SAT scores, etc.) multiracial children are not counted. But in areas of failure—child abuse, domestic violence and societal dysfunction, multiracial children and their families are counted. . . . No wonder much of the public and many professionals have a negative impression of our families" (1989).

When one begins to look at all the confusion and nomenclature, it is no wonder that multiracial children would feel some sense of identity confusion and almost "natural" that they would "do the right thing" by identifying monoracially. When society refuses to sanction you, " 'Do your own thing' is a useful metaphor to play with when the things are doing you" (as Slugoski and Ginsburg cite Wilden 1989: 48). But how has this come about? Why aren't children of more than one race described in a language that corresponds to their "more than one race" existence? Most of us accept and expect without question that there is a correlation between our language and experience. Why have we never questioned it?

The fact that multiracial people are not described in a way relative to their multiplicity undermines the idea that our language reflects the true nature of our experience. This lack of a one-to-one correspondence between our reality and our language suggests that our language as a tool has other purposes—to shape, define, control, and even obstruct our experiences. When Fanon wrote the statement at the beginning of this chapter was he thinking about what is implied by that which exists but is not expressed?

Our language serves as a vehicle through which racially mixed children understand, process, relate to, and function in their social worlds (Williams 1992). In fact, the establishment and maintenance of a socially desirable identity is perhaps its most important interpersonal goal. Hence, our language, in this view, becomes a controller of rather than merely a reactor to our social order.

By setting up a linear system with rigid monoracial descriptors, the racial identity possibilities presented to and reinforced for racially mixed children serve as a foundation from which they, and all of society as well, can conceptualize who they are, where they belong, and how they should interact in choosing and maintaining their "proper place" in society. That we have not questioned our categorization system—not to mention that it still exists in the late 1990s—is a reflection of the fact that our culture chose to make multiracial people invisible. And because of the continuous "omissions" in our system we have internalized their invisibility and reinforce this control over and over again.

We may cause ambivalence in the interracial child by supporting certain activities in schools, which act as shapers of racial identity in children. Particularly, the schools become agents of transmitting racial identity through their instruments of racial categorization.

INSTRUMENTS OF RACIAL IDENTITY

> Sociology is a rhetorical activity.
>
> —Paul Atkinson

Since the passage of the Civil Rights Act in 1964, public schools have been required by state and federal governments to submit the ethnic/racial data of every student they enroll. In order to control inconsistencies in how students would be classified, the government instituted Statistical Policy Directive 15, the ultimate authority for racial/ethnic data, including census and public school forms. It classifies race according to four racial and one ethnic category: American Indian/Alaskan Native, Asian/Pacific Islander, Black, White and an ethnic category to indicate Hispanic origin or not of Hispanic origin. Also, it requires that respondents check only one box for their ancestry ("check one box only") and "other" was not one of the categories. In the 1990 census, I, along with many parents from the multiracial community, wrote in "multiracial" or "other" and checked all races that applied to my family. Some refused to check any of the categories. This resulted in a visit by a census taker to obtain the standard monoracial response. I remember his frustration at my refusal to comply. Census policy then mandated that only the first race or ethnicity be counted. My guess is that my husband and children are probably counted as Asian since it is the first one in alphabetical order.

Thus, racially mixed individuals cannot be counted except monoracially on any government or school forms. If one refuses to check any races or checks them all, "The category which most closely reflects the individual's recognition in his community should be used for purposes of reporting on persons who are of mixed racial and/or ethnic origins" (see Appendix B.1). This instituted the "eye ball test" for racial recording that was widely practiced in schools. Should students or their parents refuse to report or check more than one racial option, school officials were empowered by federal policy to make the decisions for them.

These standards, which have been used for almost two decades, are now under review due to protests from members of the multiracial movement. These protests have been spearheaded since the late 1970s by parents who have acted individually on behalf of their mixed race children, by such groups as the American Association of Multi-Ethnic Americans (AMEA) and Project Race (Reclassify All Children Equally), a group whose express purpose is to add a multiracial category to Directive 15.

In 1994, the Office of Management and Budget (OMB) held public hearings in Boston, Denver, San Francisco, and Hawaii so that groups and individuals could voice their concerns. At the request of the AMEA, I addressed the committee in Boston on the issue of racial categorization and the schools. After listening to many individuals focus their arguments on the monoracial language of Directive 15 and the need for a multiracial category, I decided to present more tangible evidence on how this government mandate has resulted in everyday school practices, such as the lack of information, training, and resources about the multiracial experience.

Although activist members from multiracial community groups are fighting for a multiracial category, they do not have the political force to exert their influence in Congress over resistance from more established minority organizations. While these multiracial organizations have a number of dedicated individuals that have persisted in their fight to empower the multiracial community, they lack sufficient funds to operate more effectively. Consequently, they lack longevity as organized communities, and recognition and power to change their situation. These community groups remain largely ignored by society. Although multiracial organizations are in the process of gaining permanent status, it remains to be seen how successful they will be in affecting legislation. But as the incidence of interracial marriages and relationships increases "as we have seen in the 1990s," this group has the potential to become a more important American cultural and political force.

AGENTS OF RACIAL IDENTITY

One has only to think about the simple contradiction in the fact that children "of more than one race" are still being categorized in the schools as if they were "of only one" race to surmise that the role that the schools play in the identity formation of interracial children needs to be critically analyzed, and indeed radically changed. The fact that such practices were formulated at all and are still being perpetuated in the schools without question leads to a whole host of questions about the complex interconnections between the construction of identity and the cultural context in which it is framed and still being maintained. The questions that such a contradiction pose compel us to investigate racial categorization procedures in a wider context, as a particular representation of the dominant culture.

According to Giroux and other radical theorists, educators are just beginning to realize the relationships between school practices and the dominant culture, and the transformation of that culture. "The cutting edge of this perspective is its insistence on connecting macro forces in the larger society to micro analysis such as classroom studies" (Giroux 1988: 27). Furthermore, Giroux cites Michael Apple, who asks a series of questions pertinent to our analysis: "Why and how [are] the particular aspects of the collective culture . . . presented in schools as objective, factual knowledge? How concretely may official knowledge represent ideological configurations of the dominant interests in a society? How do schools legitimate

these limited and partial standards of knowing as unquestioned truths?" (1988: 27)

Against the traditional claim that the schools were only instructional sites, radical critics point to the importance of the
transmission and reproduction of a dominant culture in the
schools. They illuminate the ways in which the schools' official
practices might provide a template for other informal procedures or aspects of the "hidden curriculum"; that is, language
used, teachers' attitudes, curricula, resources, rituals, and
other informal methods might mirror that template and be possibly more important than the formal curricula. Such practices
are viewed as the effect of wider social "forms" often imposed
on a culture, which radical pedagogy insists must be analyzed
in order to understand that culture. According to Spindler,
"People can transmit culture without knowing that they do so.
Probably more culture is transmitted this way than with conscious intent" (1967: 283).

Many educators have noted these concerns. Bennet discusses
the current multicultural education movement as aiming to
achieve equity of educational opportunity. "It aims to transform
the total school environment especially the hidden curriculum,
e.g., teachers' attitudes and expectations" (1986: 14). Freire
suggests a critical pedagogy in which there is an interrogation
of the "official curriculum" of the schools: "For transformation,
we need first of all to understand the social context of teaching,
and then ask how this context distinguishes liberating education from traditional methods" (1987: 33) McLaren suggests an
examination of the schools as a ritual performance. "Rituals
may be perceived as carriers of cultural codes that shape students' perceptions and ways of understanding; they inscribe
both the 'surface structure' and 'deep grammar' of school culture" (1986: 26).

Yet, the curious and powerful question is how and why the
current multicultural education movement missed this serious
inequity concerning interracial children. While one may argue
that such an oversight is unimportant since racial categorization systems are merely school rituals that are meant to be
ignored and therefore are meaningless, germane to my interest
in undertaking this investigation is the understanding that

"rituals symbolically transmit societal and cultural ideologies, and that it is possible to know how ideologies do their 'work' by examining the key symbols and root paradigms of the ritual system" (McLaren 1986: 26).

Could educational scholars and teachers unknowingly transmit unquestioned attitudes, norms, and beliefs that seriously inhibit the very ideas of the pluralistic principles they propose by classroom practices? Such omissions, and their interconnectedness to the omissions in our school racial categorizations, need to be examined in the context of their omissions in wider society.

Thus, the schools as institutions that transmit perceptions about interracial children through both formal and informal procedures, through both conscious and unconscious means, must be carefully analyzed in all their "cultural forms" in order to reveal whether or not the schools transmit a positive racial identity for interracial children. Furthermore, in order for educators to correct their perceptions they need to be empowered to do so by confronting the sociopolitical forces in which such inequities are rooted so that subsequent changes in pedagogical practices could become, in fact, effective tools for transmitting positive identities to multiracial children.

CLASSIFICATORY THEORETICAL THOUGHT

In order to understand the true nature and meaning of what occurs in the categorization process and how this affects how interracial children are perceived, we need to understand how our nation employs the language of classificatory procedures to help shape identity for them. Meaning is derived in this approach, less in the consciousness of social actions than in the forms of language as a central force in revealing hidden meaning and in interpreting our experiences. Giroux is worth quoting at length on this subject:

One of the most important elements at work in the construction of experience and subjectivity in the schools is language. In this case, language intersects with power in the way particular linguistic forms structure and legitimate the ideologies of specific groups. Intimately related to power, language functions to both position and constitute the way that teachers and students define, mediate and understand their relation to each other, school knowledge, the institute of schooling and the larger society. (1988: 30)

Therefore, the question, "Why are children of more than one race classified on the basis of only one race?" points not only to how language does not reflect the true nature of the experience but to how language can define and obstruct the ordering of our perceptions. To answer our question one might begin to look at how such a practice could be rooted in supporting the ideologies of the dominant culture. If monoracial language is used, then how society perceives and services their needs will reflect this taxonomy of society and not that of children of multiple races.

At issue is whether the formal language of our racial categorization system suppresses any questions the dominant culture finds too difficult to raise about the complex interconnections between what the schools teach and the sociopolitical pressures that the multiracial child feels. And are multiracial children positioned into bearing the cross for the difficulties this nation faces about its own confused racial identity? How would a linguistic change in this racial ordering upset those currently benefitting from its current system of ordering their racial experience? By making interracial children visible, what problems do we pose for society by creating a voice for affirming their multiple status? How do we even talk about race unless we speak in very race-specific terms?

Durkheim and Mauss (1903), who first insisted on the social foundation of classificatory logic, concluded that classification systems were not innate but were instead products of society is fundamental to the notion that humans classify as they are taught to classify. Mary Douglas stresses that our institutions classify information that shapes our thinking, does our thinking, and maintains the "correctness" of our thinking. "To know how to resist the classifying pressures of our institutions, we would like to start an independent classificatory exercise. Unfortunately, all the classifications that we have for our thinking are provided ready-made, along with our social life. For thinking about society, we have at hand the categories we use as members of society speaking to each other about ourselves. These actors' categories work at every possible level" (1986: 99).

Furthermore, Lincoln, who also wrote of classification as an effective instrument of society, speaks of the "tyranny of taxonomy" that is, its power in a broader sense for the construction, deconstruction, and reconstruction of society itself. "Insofar as taxonomies are also instruments for the organization of society, those patterns are extended to better—yet, imposed upon—social groupings . . . within this system, age and gender, as well as race function as taxonomizers, that is, each one establishes an act of discrimination through which all members of a given class are assigned to one of two subclasses: those who possess the trait or property in question, and those who do not" (1989: 223).

Thus, how multiracial children are perceived in the schools is controlled by the language and other classification systems sanctioned by society to describe them. In this approach, language functions to both position and constitute the way teachers and students define, mediate, and understand their relation to each other and to the larger society. Mixed race children are in between classification systems that need to be carefully analyzed and revised since interracial children are constantly in the process of restructuring their racial identity and such classification systems contribute to and shape their ambivalence.

How the schools and society classify interracial children might also affect teachers' perceptions of them. Teachers may unconsciously transmit confused identities to interracial children. The language used, or the *lack of language* used, to describe children of more than one race can grant a certain amount of persuasiveness to how they are perceived. By packaging informal, printed documents, such as official school forms, they become "cultural wisdom"—thus, sanctioning how multiracial children are to be perceived by teachers and their peers. The judgments of others are used as information in categorizing ambiguous stimuli which would reflect upon teachers' perceptions and ultimately how interracial children see themselves.

If the schools are to transmit positive racial identities to mixed race children, society will have to alter how it perceives them. Although Douglas suggested that while categories are rigid and cannot be easily modified, neither can they be ignored. "They cannot neglect the challenge of aberrant forms. Any given system of classification must give rise to anomalies, and any given culture must confront events which seem to defy its assumptions. It cannot ignore the anomalies which its scheme produces" (1986: 139).

Multiracial children are a visible symbol of society's racial divisions and ambiguities. Monoracial categorization procedures reflect these inconsistencies and contradictions, which the official tenets and unofficial practices in our schools uphold, if unknowingly. A critical analysis of these procedures in our schools would reveal whether or not the schools might be limiting multiracial children to monoracial identities that could become problematic for some of them. Society has the potential to marginalize interracial children by making them invisible so that they are ignored. It is necessary to know if this is happening because it is not healthy for them or for the rest of society. Also, multiracial individuals as a group are growing in numbers and constitute a potential force to challenge racial categorization procedures in the schools as part of its hidden agenda.

We need to identify the "identity relevant explanatory speech" (Slugoski and Ginsburg 1989) that is implemented by our schools' racial categorization and is used to confine multiracial children to monoracial identity possibilities. Our language of "one race only" has become the sanctioned device used to describe multiracial children, a device that is shared and transformed by most members of our society. This linguistic "tool" is most effective for it does not stand alone; it has numerous "reinforcers" in the culture, which are presumed to be shared by all members of that culture, thus insuring its control through a continuous array of devices embedded in our institutions, especially the schools. Our schools' monoracial system for categorizing multiracial children mirrors other aspects of school culture that impede their multiracial identity. We must examine those categorizations (and our categorizations "of omission" as well) that have pervaded our attitudes about multiracial children. We must examine the categorizations that surface in a multitude of situations built into our school culture and contribute to the racial and cultural ambivalence of the multiracial child.

4

How Our School and Federal Documents Frame Racial Identity

Ethnic identity is twin skin to my linguistic identity—I am my language.

—Gloria Anzaldua

The most obvious example of how society exercises its potential to transmit confused identities to multiracial children in the schools can be evidenced through a school's implementation of its racial categorization policy by way of its instruments—school forms and other data-collecting tools. These are the printed tools that are used in the schools to implement the foundation of our nation's racial/social order. The school forms that so blatantly reinforce monoracial identity while ignoring multiple racial identity serve as very strong symbols of how our nation thinks about race and how, in effect, the nation licenses the schools to ignore the needs of multiracial children.

According to a study of the National Center for Education Statistics, about 55 percent of all public schools collect racial/ethnic data and 41 percent report that there are students for whom our standard racial categories are not accurate. Also, 73 percent of our schools limit their descriptions to the standard five categories, and about half of the remaining 27 percent who use additional categories reported that their central offices transpose these categories to correspond to the standard five categories. About 35 percent of the schools reported that when trying to decide where to put these students, they distributed them among the standard five "based on which one the school considers most appropriate" (U.S. Dept. of Education 1996: iii). Approximately one quarter of public schools (almost half in the Northeast, 44 percent) reported that the assigned teacher or administrator made the decision based on observation (better know as eyeballing) to choose which racial/ethnic category their students fit.

The tabulation and codification of multiracial children in our schools on the basis of "one race only" is a visible symbol that acts as a foundation for a much wider array of experiences and situations that maintain the "invisibility" of mixed race children in our schools. First it is through these forms that children of multiple races, as well as the rest of society, have a monoracial identity defined, legitimized, and chosen for them. Second, such instruments by way of their "language of omission" make children of mixed races "invisible." This invisibility results in a lack of affirmation for their multiple heritage and thus, awareness and concern for their unique needs. Third, it is on the basis of these forms that the government mandates school resources and materials that have a powerful and direct bearing on other "hidden curricula" of school culture that govern teacher-student interactions within the classroom.

According to a number of researchers (Douglas 1986; Giroux 1987; Lincoln 1989), drawing on impressions from theorists from the cultural-historical school, personality develops through relations to other human beings, relations that are mediated by language. Language is the ultimate form of social intercourse. It is the tool and the medium through which people gain influence over the behavior of others and over their own comprehension of those actions. Rather than being tied to particular situations, language extends beyond the particular context in which it is framed. According to Fleck, "Cognition is the most socially conditioned activity of man and knowledge is the paramount social creation. The very structure of language presents a compelling philosophy characteristic of that community, and even a single word can represent a complex theory" (cited in Douglas 1986: 12). It is through language that people internalize the attitudes of the social group and, on this basis, form their subjective attitudes about themselves in their relationship to others.

It is only in language that such a general, impersonal standpoint can be communicated against which individuals can react to their own selves and organize their responses accordingly. This is because language itself is an impersonal, social system that provides individuals with a thoroughly objective standpoint through which they may become objects to themselves. The interpretation of one's own responses, therefore, does not always reveal to us the meaning of an action in any direct terms, for the responses of the self can only enter consciousness when an individual gains an objective view of his or her own self. This can only be attained by language, by taking the language and thus an attitude of others toward the self.

But where does language come from and who or what shapes how it is constructed? If our words are not necessarily directly related to the true nature or objective reality of that which they describe, to what are they related in a direct sense? A number of researchers clarify the extent to which thinking itself is dependent upon institutions (Douglas 1986; Giroux 1988; Slugoski and Ginsburg 1989; Rose 1989). In this way, institutions that are controlled by the dominant culture use language as a tool to control how we think about things (even before we begin to think that we are thinking about it) in order to ensure that our thinking will reflect the goals of the dominant culture.

In this way, our monoracial system prevents us from thinking of multiracial children as multiracial. In fact, it is as if the language of society is at first speaking a different language from the inner language of the individual until the inner language achieves legitimacy (Douglas 1986). Even the single word "multiracial" or any other language of racial mixture that combines rather than divides us racially and in so doing acknowledges sameness among multiple races is threatening to a society that either 1) intentionally first created the idea of racial sameness/differentness and wants to remain inflexible in its racial divisions to keep the races "pure," particularly the White races, or 2) has become so entangled in its own language that it does not know how to unlock its own mindset and thus unintentionally and continuously reinforces monoracial perceptions. In this way, we formulate our "own" perceptions by carrying the social orders around in our heads and projecting them onto nature even before we can grasp that we are perceiving anything at all.

Language, in this way, acts like a web that is reinforced by an array of other sociocultural forms, such as rituals, traditions and the media, all of which influence our everyday interactions so that we are positioned to perceive the way we are instructed rather than the way the situation really "is" in reality. What is different, while it may be the opposite of sameness, is a concept that can be altered should society need that they appear to be the same. It can occur even before we can recognize it. Douglas speaks of turning the individual's mind over to an automatic pilot light (1986: 13).

But how could this happen? How is an idea seemingly different from the innate nature of things constructed so that we perceive sameness? What makes it appear to be so directly and logically related to differentness and then achieve legitimacy as sameness? Douglas (1986) is worth quoting at length on this subject:

> Where does sameness reside? The answer has to be that sameness is conferred on the mixed bundle of items that count as members of a category; their sameness is conferred and fixed by institutions. (53)

> Constructing sameness is an essential intellectual activity that goes unobserved. . . . To recognize a class of things is to polarize and exclude. It involves drawing boundaries. To move from recognizing degrees of difference to creating a similarity class is a big jump. (60)

The school, as an institution that assumes one of the most powerful influences over our children's perceptions, is licensed by us to control how our children think. Such institutions by codifying and tabulating for our reference two very different ideas (e.g., multiple races and one race as if they were the same) have put our already "ready-made" uncertainties under their control and erased their difference (Douglas 1986). Then, once multiracial children are positioned with monoracial children, we begin to see them in a very different manner than before— the same as monoracial individuals—and start to reinforce this new view in our thinking and actions. We begin to think that they really do belong with those of one race and start regrouping them with this group everytime we fill out official forms that do not give us other options. Thus, perceiving multiracial children monoracially becomes so automatic to us that we acknowledge, we reinforce, and we co-institutionalize the practice. Therefore, we need to look at the schools as an institution that confers monoracial sameness on mixed race children and sets the stage for possibly transmitting confused identities to them. We need to uncover how such expressions of difference are implicated in various expressions of knowledge and power, such as language and other sign systems that position subjects within specific webs of possibility in the schools (Giroux 1988).

In order to investigate whether or not school practices ultimately affect how mixed race children view their racial identity, I conducted research in two school systems in Massachusetts: one urban and one suburban. I wanted to find out what I suspected to be true, that urban environments might provide a more informed arena for interracial children. By examining the practices in these diverse environments, I sought to determine how both school and federal documents could possibly affect school practices for a wider range of students.

Hence, in order to understand how interracial children have been racially categorized in the schools, I will critically analyze all the printed and written materials that exhibit those categorizations. This includes school forms and federal documents, other printed materials, and memos that are utilized by our school and federal institutions to explain the intent of those documents and the appropriate manner for answering the questions on racial categorization. I will illustrate how our language is a language of identity. Those simple technical procedures for defining racial identity and tabulating those forms wipe out and neatly reshape the difference inherent in the racial identity of multiracial children to make them fit our monoracial code for acceptable racial identity behavior. Since many of these documents are redundant, many have been eliminated even though their inclusion might bear testimony to how our written forms consistently create and reinforce how we should perceive the identity of mixed race children. Thus, the representative sample of documents provided in this text mirror a countless number of additional documents that instruct us to think that the multiracial child not only "ought" to be perceived as monoracial but "is" monoracial.

Additionally, before this book went to press, the documental analysis was updated and comparisons were often noted about how the same issue is viewed over time. These changes illustrate that the process by which we categorize our mixed race individuals is still an evolving one. The quest to have multiracial individuals' racial identity affirmed by the American public is still in process. However, this does not mean that any issue that has been altered today or tomorrow will immediately set off an automatic pilot to alter what the American public believes about mixed race individuals. Changing how people think is a slow and difficult process. Hence, the old forms still bear witness to how our perceptions have been constructed and reinforced historically in such a way that they will be sustained for a long period of time.

SCHOOL FORMS

School Registration Forms

Approximately 55 percent of all public schools nationally collect and tabulate racial/ethnic data when students initially register for school and another 17 percent also collect these data whenever students change schools within the district (U.S. Dept. of Education 1996). Thus, this simple form marks for most parents of multiracial children an introduction into the schools' racial/social ordering (see Appendix A.1). In Massachusetts, all school systems have registration forms—one for each elementary, junior, and senior high—in which students are categorized racially, for example, using the statement "Please circle which one category best represents your child's race." In response to pressure from the multiracial community, of late some towns around the country have added a "multiracial" or "other" category. But, this is not recorded on state tallies since such responses must be changed to fit one of the sanctioned, five monoracial categories; and therefore, technically, they still don't exist as mixed race students. They are most often unaware that the race that they choose (or ultimately are forced to "accept") is codified to fit one racial category, then tabulated and kept as part of the schools' racial statistics, which affect how money and awareness is allocated on local, state, and federal levels.

Some Suggestions for Collecting and Using Racial Statistics

This is a memo distributed by the Massachusetts Department of Education to school personnel, particularly principals, as guidelines for filling in the Individual School Report, which is the school census submitted by October 1 of every year. The 1990 memo states that traditionally the Individual School Report has been conducted by the principal or teachers in each school, who eyeball each classroom and report the numbers of students in each racial category. No record has been kept of which students were in each category, with the result that some students have been counted in different ways at different times. A number of towns now use the school's registration form as a basis for deciding what race should be declared for the child, thus seemingly putting the power to decide in the hands of the parents who fill out the registration form.

For example, this memo suggests when a new file is being created that a determination of race be made by the school administrator/secretary. It suggested gathering information from an "optional form" to be filled out by parents or students when registering for school:

Dear Parent,

Under state law we must report the racial enrollment at each school to assure that students are not denied any right or benefit because of their race. If you choose, you may identify your child according to the following categories: American Indian, Black (not Hispanic), Asian, Hispanic (nonwhite), Hispanic (white), and White. If you do not choose to do so, we will use our best judgment. This information will not be available as part of the school system's records on any individual student. . . . School officials are both allowed and required to identify the students by race if the parents do not.

What is interesting about this memo is the careless use of the words "chose" and "optional." Is there a choice? Is this really optional? What kind of choice is it for parents who choose not to comply with categorization procedures that they consider erroneous about the race of their child?

In another section entitled, "What should you do about ambiguous cases?" principals are advised on how to report a student who has parents from different racial groups. Two examples are given: a student who has African American and Hispanic parents and a Cape Verdean student. In the case of the Black/Hispanic student it was suggested, "It would be important to know which group the student identifies with." However, in the case of the Cape Verdean student, who has mixed African and Portuguese heritage and does not tend to identify with African Americans, how he or she self-identifies was to be ignored. "Nevertheless, it would be inappropriate to identify them categorically as "White." Hence, it is clear that when a student is a composite of two minority cultures, he or she may self-identify; but, when there is a racial mixture with the White culture, this right is taken away "because this would deny Cape Verdean students protection under the law for the discrimination they experience." But what about their right to self-identify? In this report it is suggested, "Individual students and their families will be able to make those determinations if they wish; if not, school officials must use their best judgment."

This memo appears to be uncomfortable about admitting that the bottom line is to identify students of "ambiguous cases" as minorities regardless of any consideration to how they may want to self-identify. Self-identification is supported only when it does not conflict with administrators' need to have them identify. The memo states: "The issue is not color but race, and race is a matter of self-identification as much as it is appearance. This is an area in which sensitivity and good judgement are essential, and these qualities must be exercised by the principal who is directly responsible for racial identification."

There is much confusion, contradiction, and of course, ambiguity in what this memo suggests is the right thing to do in handling "ambiguous cases." On one hand, it says to identify ambiguous cases as minorities even if parents do not identify their children that way. Therefore, language that affirms self-identification is meaningless if the self-identification of any person or group is ignored even for the best reasons.

The reasons for racial categorizations, as stated in this report, are that minority groups have historically been discriminated against and that categorization assures "special protection" of which they're entitled to receive. However, it is clear that students have rights to protection only according to monoracial categorizations. "That is why, in an ambiguous case, it is preferable to report a student as being 'minority' rather than 'White'." This typifies an age-old argument against the use of the "multiracial" category. Often an additional category is perceived as taking numbers away from funding for minority groups. Such concerns precede any other concerns about the effects on services available to multiracial children or individual rights for self-identification.

I reviewed this memo again in 1996 and found no changes on how students are to be reported, but the language used was camouflaged with less disturbing images. For example, the word "eyeballing" was changed to "visually identify" and "use your best judgment." Also, there was no reference to "ambiguous" cases, but it did mention the fact that schools could create additional categories, such as "biracial," but that they must be compiled into the standard five categories for reporting purposes.

In conclusion, this memo justifies these procedures on the basis that minority students and their schools might need extra help in educational curricula and strategies and that federal and state funds should be available for them. It assumes that such an imposed racial structure and corresponding services are adequate for the multiracial child. Also, while these instructions inform administrators of their responsibilities in filing the Individual School Report, they also serve to legitimize for them the "proper procedures" that should be used in all racial tallying in the schools. It is also obvious that the template for these instructions is Directive 15, which will be discussed again in this chapter under government forms.

Individual School Report, Table 3: Enrollment by Grade by Race

Every school must fill out the Individual School Report by October 1 of each year (see Appendix A.2). This form is a questionnaire that is filled out by the school principal or secretary and sent to the Massachusetts Department of Education, where it is tabulated and codified before being sent to the federal government. The information for filling out the form is often taken, but not necessarily, from school registration forms filled out by parents. In the past, schools have used other methods such as visual observation. Also, the administrator who compiles this information has already been made aware of the official guidelines mentioned above before his or her responses are recorded.

This form tabulates student's racial status on the basis of six categories; however, it is significant that even these monoracial categories vary from year to year. On the 1982 form the six categories were 1. American Indian, 2. Black, 3. Asian, 4. Non-White Hispanic, 5. White Hispanic, and 6. White. It is significant that the 1996 form has five categories since all Hispanics regardless of race share the same category. It is also significant to note that Table 3 eliminates the fifth category, jumping from category four to six: 1. American Indian, 2. Black (not of Hispanic origin), 3. Asian, 4. Hispanic, and 6. White (not of Hispanic Origin). This is indicative of the inconsistencies that coding erroneously by monorace entails. This also recalls some of Mary Douglas's (1986) ideas on how sameness/differentness is created by institutions that put our uncertainties under control. So now the government has told us that all Hispanics are the same race. Yet, in the instructions that personnel school receive for filling out these forms, a "Hispanic is a person of Mexican, Puerto Rican, Cuban, Central or South American, or other Spanish culture or origin, *regardless of race*" (italics added). Is someone from Spain "not of Hispanic origin" or is he or she White?

Individual School Report (Public Summary)

In Appendix A.3 is a sample page from the public summary taken on all the racial tabulations that each town in Massachusetts has collected for the state's racial statistics from 1990 to 1996. Information for this form has been taken directly from the Individual School Report, which may or may not have utilized the school registration form as a method of gathering this information. It illustrates again the predominant philosophy of all categorization policies, that even one drop of non-White blood categorizes one as a minority regardless of other racial compositions. The school census provides a basis for tabulating our racial distribution in the schools and on this basis funding is appropriated to service the specific needs of minority children. Thus, this form ultimately makes multiracial children invisible in the schools in nearly all their programs, curricula, and other activities.

While some traditional educators might argue that schools are apolitical institutions, racial categorization procedures such as this provide us with visible evidence of how the schools suppress difference and shape monoracial identity, a state of affairs that might be rather uncomfortable for some mixed race children. Giroux (1988) and other radical educators illuminate how actions such as this need to be studied. Requiring racial census taking, though not mentioned by any radical educator that I could find, is a school policy that influences how multiracial children see themselves racially.

But why do we create these categories? Where do they come from? Douglas asks some questions pertinent to our analysis:

Are we using an exhausting set of public categories on which the logical operations are performed? Are they the right categories for our questions? What does the rightness of categories mean? And apart from those we have put into an analysis, what should we say about the ones we have left out? What about other social orders that might have been that did not come into existence? (1986: 70)

Thus, this policy of racial census taking has silenced the multiracial voice by making mixed race children invisible in the schools and validating their existence if and only if they are monoracial. This form is very important because it provides the basis for legitimizing the omission of their true multiracial identity, and this practice permeates their total school environment and informs almost all of their experiences.

What is also most significant about the Individual School Report is the presence it creates in our minds, and more importantly in the minds of administrators, by its very powerful codifications and tabulations. That is, once the image is framed to transmit the parameters of our racial identity order, our schools reinforce this concept of sameness and make its existence practicable. Rose, clarifying some of the principles of Foucault, speaks of the understanding of such codifications as "techniques for the disciplining of human indifference": "Such calculative practices are not auto-effective. Vocabularies of calculation and accumulation of information go hand in hand with the development of "techniques by which the outcome of calculative practices—in the form of decisions as to what should be done—can be translated into action upon the objects of calculation" (1989: 121). Thus, by enumerating the school population racially, those who have an inner and quieter multiracial voice are further silenced and disciplined while those who are monoracial are validated and reinforced in public situations and practice.

Standardized Tests

Third and fifth graders were administered the Massachusetts Basic Skills Testing Program (see Appendix A.4) during the 1990–91 school year and fourth, eighth, and tenth graders were given the Massachusetts Educational Assessment Program (MEAP) tests in 1996. Students are asked to fill out their own tests under the background information section. In 1990–91 the students were asked to fill in the circle corresponding to the the following, "You are: Black (not Hispanic), White (not Hispanic), Asian, Hispanic, and Other." On the later test, though the terminology is changed for some groups, it remained the same for interracial children. I was not able to receive a copy of this later test but was able to get some information over the phone. On the MEAP test, students are asked, "Which best describes you?" The new categories are: Black/African American, White, Hispanic/Latin American, Asian or Pacific Islander, and Other. What is interesting is that the terminology has been altered to reflect new awareness issues for other groups while preserving the "Other" category for interracial children. However, the "Other" category is also utilized by a number of people who do not want to identify with specific racial groups but might want to identify with cultural groups, such as Cape Verdean, Hawaiian, Haitian, etc. that are not available for identification purposes on school and government forms.

Attendance Reports

In some towns, teachers take racial attendance on a daily basis as illustrated by this school form (see Appendix A.5). It is called the "Daily Count" and tabulates attendance according to gender and race using six monoracial categories. Thus, teachers are reminded on a daily basis that their multiracial children do not exist. Also, one can assume that this form, which is already monoracially codified, is just another collection device for a larger form in which all the monoracial statistics are gathered and analyzed.

Other School Forms and Reports

Most teachers made references to a number of other forms, including students' reports, class lists, the pupil master file update forms, and the Massachusetts student master file datasheet. In addition, teachers reported that there were also a number of other forms that they routinely used or administered.

Chapter 622 Regulations from the Massachusetts Department of Education

Chapter 622 Regulations Pertaining to Access to Equal Educational Opportunity were adopted by the Massachusetts Board of Education on June 24, 1975, and became effective on September 1, 1975. Before this book went to press, I sought to update my printed matter and found some significant changes. Chapter 622 is now codified as Chapter 76, Section 5, and Chapter 76, Section 16. Chapter 622 and Chapter 76 were/are the official Massachusetts Department of Education policies put in effect to protect the needs of students. The previously mentioned school forms collect and tabulate data in order to enforce this policy. I will note significant changes and additions since the original form was first published. Chapter 76, Section 5 reads,

> No person shall be excluded from or discriminated against in admission to a public school of any town, or in obtaining the advantages, privileges and courses of study of such public school on account of race, color, sex, religion, national origin or sexual orientation.

It is interesting that the words "or sexual orientation" have been added to protect the rights of gay or lesbian individuals. I do feel that the present wording "of race" should be sufficient to support mixed raced individuals. However, when I think of all the mistaken assumptions made about race in a very singular fixed way, perhaps it may be necessary to add the letter "s" to the word "race," for example, "race(s)" to emphasize the inclusion of mixed race individuals. There are ten sections of the 622 Regulations. Those sections that will be analyzed because of their relevance to interracial children and that might represent possibilities for filing a grievance include Guidance, Curricula, Extra-Curricula Activities, and Active Efforts.

Guidance Section 26.04 (Item 3) reads:

> No materials or tests shall be employed for guidance purposes which discriminate and/or limit choices on the basis of race, color, sex, religion or national origin.

Both school materials and tests discriminate against interracial children. Interracial children on school tests must "choose one box only" when filling out biographical data; thus they limit choices for them on the basis of race. In school materials, interracial children are not mentioned. Guidance counselors do not have materials for them. The materials they do have are for monoracial students only, thus limiting choices on the basis of race. This issue will be discussed more comprehensively in the next chapter when I discuss teacher perceptions of how school culture shapes racial identity.

Curricula Section 26.05 (Item 1) reads:

> The curricula of all public school systems shall present in fair perspective the culture, history, activities and contributions of persons and groups of different races, nationalities, sexes and colors.

Racially mixed persons are not acknowledged in all these areas according to the data collected for this project.

Curricula Section 26.05 (Item 2) reads:

> All school books, instructional and educational materials shall be reviewed for sex-role and minority group stereotyping. Appropriate activities, discussions and/or supplementary materials shall be used to counteract the stereotypes depicted in such materials.

All school books reinforce minority stereotyping when they reinforce that all minorities chose to identify monoracially. All school books should be reviewed for monoracial group stereotyping. Interracial children are omitted in school books, instructional and educational materials, class discussions and/or supplementary materials. They are practically invisible in all cultural transformations in the schools. In contrast, interracial children are subjected to situations in which a monoracial perspective is reinforced, including most multicultural activities. Such activities bear with them a measure of legitimacy, thus contributing to identity ambivalence in some children who might feel uncomfortable and/or silenced by such monoracial stereotyping. Monoracial stereotyping exists at psychic cost to the students who are uncomfortable with not identifying with all parts of their racial identity.

Curricula Section 26.05 (Item 3) reads:

> Schools books, instructional and educational materials purchased after the date of these regulations shall, in the aggregate, include characteristics and situations which depict individuals of both sexes and minority groups in a broad variety of positive roles.

School books should eliminate monoracial biases and include characteristics and situations that depict individuals of multiracial groups in a broad variety of roles.

Extra-Curricula Activities, Section 26:06 (Item 8) reads:

> When offering extra-curricula programs, schools shall take into consideration the ethnic traditions of the student body. Criteria not related to skill levels which act to exclude members of *one* sex or any racial, religious or ethnic group represented in the school from participation in specific athletic or other extra-curricular activities cannot be permitted.

This section primarily concerned itself with sports activities and especially devoted most of its attention to protecting equality in women's sports. In fact equality of women in sports is mentioned in just about all eight of its articles in very explicit ways. It is obvious that the authors of Chapter 622 saw the need to be very explicit when addressing issues of equality of women in sports, rather than simply stating in general terms as they do about race. It was obvious to them that the words "on the basis of race, sex, or national origin" (the words "sexual orientation," though recently added elsewhere, were omitted here) were not sufficient to protect the rights of women athletes.

All school programs and activities highlight monoracial traditions without acknowledging that some students might have multiple racial traditions. While this may be seem like a point taken too far since many students, including monoracial students, can have multiple ethnic traditions, I do not believe such is the case. Since we have been so fixed-race based as a nation, this notion has also affected how we think about our ethnic traditions, which also suffer from the notion that we are of singular ethnic/racial backgrounds. Each school I studied had clubs for students who identified with one race/culture only. In fact, I spoke to some parents of interracial children who felt unwanted when seeking to join some groups for minority students.

Active Efforts, Section 26.08 (Item 3) reads:

It shall be the responsibility of the school committee and the superintendent to provide necessary information and in-service training for all school personnel in order to . . . advance means of achieving educational goals in a manner free from discrimination on account of race, color, sex, religion or national origin . . . enhance consciousness of the kinds of discriminatory and prejudicial practices and behavior which may occur in the public schools.

Active Efforts, Section 26.08 (Item 4) reads:

The superintendent, as an agent of the school committee, shall promote and direct effective procedures for the full implementation of these regulations, and shall make recommendations to the committee for the necessary policies, program changes and budget resources allocations to achieve adherence to these regulations.

There is no significant example of school personnel's awareness of the unique needs of the racially mixed child in the schools, especially in the most vital area that affects students, that is, in the immediate consciousness of the school personnel who determine the practices and activities in the schools. Interracial children are practically nonexistent in all teacher training programs and in other in-service programs for school personnel.

FEDERAL DOCUMENTS

Directive No. 15

Race and Ethnic Standards for Federal Statistic and Administrative Reporting, Statistical Policy Handbook, U.S. Dept. of Commerce, 1978, Office of Management and Budget (OMB) includes Directive No. 15 (see Appendix B.1). This directive provides guidelines for record keeping of data on race and ethnicity in federal program reporting and statistical activities. Directive 15 outlines definitions according to five monoracial categories: American Indian, Asian or Pacific Islander, Black, Hispanic, and White. In fact it specifically states: "The category which most closely reflects the individual's recognition in his community should be used for purposes of reporting on persons who are of mixed racial and/or ethnic origins." It is interesting that racial identification by community recognition rather than by the self is upheld. It is also interesting to note what the directive states about additional categories:

> In no case should the provisions of this Directive be construed to limit the collection of data to the categories described above. However, any reporting required which uses more detail shall be organized in such a way that the additional categories can be aggregated into these basic racial/ethnic categories. . . . Any variation which cannot be aggregated into the basic categories will have to be specifically approved by the Office of Federal Statistical Policy and Standards.

OMB Directive 15 is still the ultimate authority for racial/ethnic classifications on all government forms, including classifications on all public school forms. Efforts to change school forms to include a multiracial category have come up against this directive in that they have been forced to restrict the use of the multiracial classifications to internal, non-federal uses only, which bear little significance *(AMEA Networking News*

1993). For example, as this goes to press, many schools are including a multiracial category particularly in the school registration forms that are usually filled out by parents. However, this is merely a symbolic gesture and does not bear any weight on government forms and possibly other school forms in which race is a factor. Recently a bill was presented in the Massachusetts Legislature that mandated the inclusion of a multiracial category on the forms used by institutions of public education and employment. Of the bill's fifteen lines, nine mandated the new "multiracial" category and disallowed the use of the word "other." The remaining six lines undid all that the first nine lines advocated by allowing a rejection of the new category by the federal government. "Such individuals shall be redesignated by allocating them to racial or ethnic classifications approved by the federal agency" (De Leo 1997).

Hence, Directive 15 has stonewalled any attempt to add a multiracial category in a way that is accountable to its people. In telephone calls to the U.S. Department of Education, Office for Civil Rights, I found that while additional categories are appearing on school registration forms across the country, multiracial students will still be categorized and therefore counted as minorities on the federal level. "OMB Directive 15 forces government agencies to make unconstitutional demands of multiracial/multiethnic individuals by

1. requiring them to give false information on official forms;
2. invading their personal privacy right to their actual identity;
3. invading the privacy of multiethnic families by interfering with the child-parent relationship, that is, by requiring a child to deny the ethnicity of one or the other of her/his parents;
4. invading the privacy and equal protection rights of individuals, particularly public school children, by subjecting them to a so-called visual inspection procedure to which members of no other populations are subject; and
5. denying them the benefits and civil rights protections

which other people enjoy by virtue of being counted specifically." (Fernandez, quoted in *Interracial Voice*, January 29, 1996)

Collection of Racial and Ethnic Data, and Answers

Even though this memo from the Office for Civil Rights, Department of Health and Human Services is not of an educational institution, it is significant for two reasons. It again shows the effect of Directive 15 and it also illustrates that racial categorization on forms is neither optional nor a validation of a person's right to self-identify, even though the form specifically states that it is optional to self-identify. Furthermore, the memo once again demonstrates the entanglements that are encountered when one tries to be consistent in enforcing an illogical idea. The memo reads:

> Self-identification is the preferred method. If the information is not provided by self-identification, the collector may record the information through observation alone; the information collector may not second-guess or change a self-declaration unless such a declaration is patently false.

Who decides what is "patently false"? It is clear that the responsibility and power for whether an individual can racially self-identify rests with the collection agent rather than with the individual. Thus, self-identification is the preferred method, if and only if the collector prefers it. This is another example of the inconsistences generated by the illogical monoracial mandates of Directive 15. As it will be noted in a later document compiled by the same agency, the Office of Management and Budget specifically states: "Self-identification is not the preferred method" (see Appendix B.2).

Race and Ethnic Standards for Statistics and Administrative Reporting

This report by Katherine Wallman, Statistical Policy Division, Office of Management and Budget, and John Hodgon, Office for Civil Rights, Department of Health, Education and Welfare (July 1977), is the output of a task force, Federal Interagency Committee on Education (FICE), which prepared racial categories and definitions for federal statistics and administrative reporting. What mandated this task force was that agencies such as educational institutions were reporting in their racial and ethnic data minor differences in their categories and definitions. This resulted in an increased burden and noncompatibility of data across federal agencies. It also illustrates the mayhem federal agencies encounter when trying to enforce something so illogical as monoracial categorization.

In the section entitled "Use of Self-Identification to Obtain Racial and Ethnic Data," the problem of how to deal with those who object to placing themselves in one of five mutually exclusive categories, none of which appears appropriate, is addressed. It is noted that this situation applies particularly to persons of mixed racial or ethnic backgrounds who might be more amenable to identifying in a sixth category—"other."

3. Agencies may include an "Other (specify)" category for self-identification by respondents who feel that none of the five categories adequately describes their heritage. This sixth category should be added, however, only when the data gathering agency is prepared to assign the persons choosing this response option to a standard category for purposes of presenting aggregated information. While the use of the "other" category is admittedly cumbersome, it appears preferable to allow its use in cases where such an option may serve to increase response rate and minimize respondent concern. It should be emphasized that the use of an "Other (specify)" category is permissible only in cases where respondent self-identification is used; this option is not to be used in reporting forms which collect racial and ethnic data through observer identification of such characteristics.

It would appear, based on the wording of this memo, that the use of the word "other" is used to soothe objections to the restrictive categories and to mask the fact that the racially mixed individual who chooses to self-identify as "other" is still recorded in one of the standard categories. That this "other" is meaningless in the eyes of federal reporting of racial statistics is obvious.

It is also important to analyze what we say when we refer to people as "Other." When we use the word "other," it identifies the person as outside yourself and different from you. But the person who decides who is "other" is the assessor or in this case, also the collector empowered with making the judgment that this group of people is marginal—not just different, but different in an ambiguous kind of way. For if our documents, as a cultural form that sanctions only five distinct and separate groups, define those who combine these groups as "other," they position them as being of ambiguous status, at best. This reminds me of a mother who explained that the descriptive "other" made her feel that her child was from "outer space."

Corrigan (1989: 74) recalls Focault's thoughts about how our "descriptives operate as both prescriptions—(the totalizing 'ought' of normalizations) and inscriptions—the individualizing 'is' of identifications" (Focault 1982). When we use descriptors such as "other" to describe those with multiple racial heritages, with the knowledge that such descriptors are a substitute for the more "legitimate" categories, we suggest that they ought to be perceived in a marginal sort of way. And when we inscribe such descriptors in our documents, the significance abruptly changes from how they "ought" to be perceived to an expression of what "is" perceived, reinforced as a universal norm for our reference.

The word "other," once viewed as a viable solution to the "problem" of how to classify "them," is not acceptable to most members of the multiracial community, but it is still being presented in our federal documents as a possibility. Note the following document, which reviewed Direcitve 15.

OMB Standards for the Classification of Federal Data on Race and Ethnicity

This federal register notice, published in August of 1995, was the result of the public hearings that took place in three cities in July of 1994, during which Directive 15 was reviewed (see Appendix B.2). These hearings were a response to the increased criticism and pressure on the government to have the directive amended. This process of review of Directive 15 is meant to end in late 1997, when the OMB publishes its final decision regarding any changes in a *Federal Register* notice. Significant are the following issues addressed: self-identification versus third-party identification, the possibility of eliminating all classifications of persons by race and ethnicity, and the possibility of identifying multiracial individuals.

This document also makes a startling omission concerning the use of self-identification: "*Self-identification is not the preferred method* among federal agencies concerned with monitoring civil rights. They prefer to collect racial and ethnic data by visual observation. Since discrimination is based on the *perception* of an individual's race . . ." (italics added) (p. 44679 of document, see Appendix B.2).

Also significant are the separate suggestions in Table 1: Summary of Options for Identification of Multiracial Persons (p. 44685 of document, see Appendix B.2), which discusses the pros and cons of the various options, such as adding a "multiracial" category and "other" category for individuals of multiracial backgrounds. In introducing the options for race classifying, this document states that "how to identify individuals of more than one race is perhaps the issue that has engendered the most controversy in the present review." It outlines how Directive 15 creates a number of objections within the multiracial community.

But it never mentions the power inherent in the document itself and invested in the assessor in framing possibilities for mixed race children. In almost all cases, a monoracial category is not addressed as a cultural form that creates and constructs our thoughts. It is assumed that we own our thoughts, that they exist already rather than that they have been positioned previously by the directives mandated by our government.

I addressed OMB in Boston on July 7, 1994, at the request of the AMEA. I limited my discussion to that which I observed as a researcher and teacher in the schools and gave concrete evidence of how Directive 15 influences racial identity through school curricula, resources, materials, cultural programming, teacher perceptions, and other aspects of school culture.

Education and Title VI

This phamphlet issued by the U.S. Department of Education outlines the connection between Title VI of the Civil Rights Act of 1964 and its compliance with the U.S. Department of Education. Programs and activities that receive Department of Education funds must operate in a nondiscriminatory manner. These may include but are not limited to admissions, recruitment, financial aid, academic programs, student treatment and services, counseling and guidance, discipline, recreation, physical education, athletics, housing, and employment. This memo is important because it identifies discriminatory problems that the Office of Civil Rights has resolved in the past and therefore would be the agency that might resolve any categorization issue that affects mixed race students and services. It also outlines how to file a complaint.

However, in a conversation with personnel from this office, I determined that based on federal guidelines (Directive 15), the Department of Education did not have the jurisdiction to dispute a case against monoracial categorization. Thus, the Department of Education as "reinforcer" of our monoracial identity process illustrates how our system works to exclude multiracial children. We set up "binding barriers" that protect our monoracial culture by excluding multiracial culture from our language. Hence, our government agencies cannot protect that which does not exist. According to the current laws, which acknowledge the rights of all monoracial individuals, interracial children are not discriminated against since they are not discriminated against as a member of either one majority or minority race. The key is that multiracial language needs to be added in order for this issue to be addressed by any government agency.

For example, through a grassroots multiracial community group, I received a letter that was sent from the Office for Civil Rights of the U.S. Department of Education to a senator who had filed a complaint on behalf of a constituent complaining about public school forms requesting racial information in such a way that they discriminated against mixed race students. The letter from the Department of Education merely reshaped Directive 15. In order to cite its policy on racial categorization and public school forms, it makes reference to the following 1984 Elementary and Secondary Education Civil Rights Survey:

> RACIAL/ETHNIC CATEGORIES—Racial/ethnic designations, as used by the U.S. Department of Education, Office for Civil Rights, do NOT denote scientific definitions of anthropological origins. For the purpose of this report, a pupil may be included in the group to which he or she appears to belong, identifies with, or is regarded in the community as belonging to. However, no person should be counted in more than one racial/ethnic category. The manner of collecting the racial/ethnic information is left to the discretion of the institution provided that the system which is established results in reasonably accurate data.

The language used in this memo obviously tries to validate monoracial categorizations in subjective language that is determined by others rather than self. For example, phrases like "appears to belong" and "is regarded in the community as belonging to" are used instead of "a pupil may be included in the group to which he or she chooses to self-identify with," which deprives them of their right to self-identify. The memo continues:

> School districts are free to use any method of determining the race of particular students as long as the system used results in "reasonably accurate data." . . .
> We suggest that classroom teachers simply count the children by the racial identification that appears to best represent the child's race within the limited number of categories available.

By using the language "any method," even the antiquated practice of eyeballing a student could then be a valid method of data collection. Until the practice of forcing parents to "decide" (or they couldn't register their children) on school registration forms was instituted, the practice of eyeballing by teachers and other school personnel was the most common practice. Thus, this method would still be valid, for words such as "appears to belong," "best represent," and other visual clues empower the assessor/collector to practice eyeballing once again. It is no wonder that the federal government also needed to validate the concept of "reasonably accurate data" rather than "accurate data" or "most possible accurate data." Data is never totally accurate, however, the goal of data collection should never be to deliberately overlook a population of people and the very core of their identity.

What is of additional interest is the rationale cited in a letter from an administrator of the Office for Civil Rights in an attempt to justify such incomplete categorizations.

> the terms "biracial" and "interracial," although they may be personally preferable, would not be particularly useful to the work of OCR. . . . While the designation "biracial" might be personally significant, the term loses meaning in the context of OCR's data collection efforts, which are designed to indicate potential civil rights violations.

Hence, the Office for Civil Rights legitimizes racial categorizations on the basis of such language as "appears to belong," "is regarded in the community as belonging to," "that appears to best represent," all "within the limited number of categories available." By limiting interracial children's self-definitions to monoracial categorizations with absolute, concrete parameters that are not inclusive of their multiple identities, interracial children's rights to identify in a way that is personally preferable are denied.

I received a discrimination complaint form in the mail and spoke at length to this agency and was informed about a recent complaint from a Boston parent concerning their child's right to identify his multiple racial status. This office determined that based on their federal guidelines (Directive 15) they did not have the jurisdiction to dispute the case. This is a reinforce-

ment of how our racial discriminatory policy, which should protect the multiracial child, is limited by the official language that
makes mixed race children invisible and thus is incapable of
protecting. According to current laws, interracial children are
not discriminated against since they are not discriminated
against as a member of a majority or minority race.

CONCLUSION

On the surface, one might assume that it would be absolutely
ridiculous to imagine that all children of more than one race
can comfortably "check one box only" for their own idea of their
racial identity. However, when one adds up all the monoracial
descriptors, calculations, and other monocultural artifacts of
the "social algebra" paradigm (Corrigan 1989) that shapes and
reinforces America's "folk taxonomy of races" (Lieberman et al.
1989), including those imposed in the schools, a monoracial
identity for multiracial children seems to be quite logical. "As
would any categorization, it imposes a fictional order" (Willett
1993) that shapes their own racial idea of themselves and how
others validate their experiences for them.

Multiracial children, if indeed they have identity problems
or "ambiguous" identities, are only responding in an appropriate manner to an "inappropriate" classificatory system. If multiracial children have ambiguous identities, their definition on
school forms within very definite and concrete monoracial
terms may be a causal factor. Since there is such an obvious
contradiction between the translation from the official monoracial language of school forms and the reality of their multiracial being, and vice versa, that ambiguity and discomfort
would be natural responses.

Hence, there is no reason why a multiracial child, given the
impersonal standpoint of language and seemingly the only
valid way to reflect upon their experience, would be likely to
have a comfortable multiracial identity without the degree of
support that is already provided for other monoracial groups.
How is it possible for a child to deny an important piece of himself or herself without some discomfort? Yet, over and over on

a number of "official" school forms, multiracial children are reflecting upon imposed monoracial identity language, which they may not feel describes their inner experience.

When they are described as monoracial on school forms they experience themselves through others outside of themselves and may begin to bring into question how they view the very experience itself. Thus, even though racially mixed children may bring a sense of their multiracial experience to the classroom, they are often faced with very real situations; whereby, they are repeatedly described, codified, and forced to comply with only monoracial language possibilities to describe their experience. Through deliberate instructions on school forms that compel them to "check one race only," multiracial children are forced to legitimize a monoracial existence for themselves, which eventually becomes "their" experience through their own participation.

School personnel need to understand that current monoracial classificatory systems not only position multiracial students into discovered meanings; they also control how they actually construct meaning. Theoretical work (Spindler 1967; Giroux 1988; McLaren 1986) would suggest that multiracial students observe and analyze the real practices and events around them that interpret and therefore compose the template for their ideas about themselves (Slugoski and Ginsburg 1989). Therefore, the language of these school forms, which are used to describe them in some way, become a central force in how multiracial students interpret, in how they produce, and in how they sustain the experience of what being multiracial actually means in society.

By packaging monoracial language as "cultural wisdom" on school forms, the schools are responding, though perhaps unintentionally, to a federal misrepresentation system that ultimately controls how interracial children interpret, continue to participate in producing, and in this way, sustaining their existence. Multiracial children are not monoracial but current classification practices that legitimize that they are, are like any other mismatch—they do not fit. And attempts that appear to make multiracial students fit must distort reality in order to do so, so that they, in effect, continue to control how multiracial students respond to their experiences.

That the schools have been so successful in ordering the racial identity of multiracial students despite these discrepancies evidences the power that such organizational structures have to influence and govern the sum total of experiences or "hidden curricula" of student life for the multiracial child. Giroux believed that these organizational structures influence and govern teacher-student interactions within the classroom. "Unlike the official curriculum, with its stated cognitive and affective objectives, the hidden curriculum in this case is rooted in those organizational aspects of classroom life which are not commonly perceived by either students or teachers" (Giroux 1988: 32).

If the schools are to meet the needs of multiracial students, how students are documented will have to be altered so that multiracial children can reinterpret, re-analyze, and begin to reconstruct their experience for themselves. In addition, current procedures need to be changed and explicitly noted to protect their rights. Current language, such as "on the basis of race," which should have been sufficient, has failed to protect their needs because the public assumes rather than actualizes this recognition. Only through proper documentation can their self-definitions, self-interpretations be acknowledged, actualized, and reinforced because they exist in the system and are counted.

Whether or not this silencing of multiracial identities is intentional (to keep the races pure) or unintentional (to respect separate racial identities), the result is that whole populations are being overlooked at the very core of their racial identity. Thus the tabulations of racial identity in the schools currently discriminate against multiracial children, as will be illustrated more concretely in the next chapter.

5

How Our School Culture Frames Racial Identity

The proper role of the schools in the socialization of Afro-American, Mexican-American, Native-American, Asian-American, European-American and mainland Puerto Rican children is a matter of great concern to social scientists, educators and policy makers. . . . To improve minority education there is a need for improved curricula, better teaching and a more equitable allocation of resources. The community and the schools should work together to achieve these common goals and schools must be more responsive to diversity in American society.

—Edgar Epps

Although these words were written in 1974, it was not until the middle and late 1980s that the schools began to respond to the needs of their diverse students, that is, at least those students whose cultural identities were singular and fixed and could be acknowledged by a rigidly stratified and racially segregated society. Although multicultural education is attempting to change social order to empower a more diverse population, interracial children, who are mandated to accept being categorized on the basis of one race only, still remain statistically invisible in the schools and are thus not reflected in the everyday experiences of their schools and communities.

In order to get a glimpse into societal and school awareness about interracial children, consider what happened when I visited the main branches of two town libraries and the school library of one of the towns. When I asked the librarians if they had books about interracial children, both responded, "Of course, we do." Then they proceeded to proudly show me their books about monoracial, minority children. In the school library, the librarian looked up at me and said in a mocking tone, "I don't mean to be facetious, but we've had those books since the sixties." These incidents give one an idea of the level of understanding that I found in the institutions I visited; there was the assumption that the needs of interracial children were being met through the resources provided for monoracial minority children.

In the previous chapter, I reviewed the written language used in the schools, language that categorizes students monoracially. Could this official language used in the schools be internalized by interracial students and affect their racial self-image? I found it impossible to imagine that a racially mixed child, especially one who had been raised by both parents, would not have an identity of some sort, good or bad, comfortable or uncomfortable, as being *both* Black and White, or whatever racial combination a child might be. Is monoracial identity really "entirely possible" or even "entirely plausible" for these children, or is their multiracial identity just suppressed by a very racially confused nation and implemented by the schools?

It became important to me to find out about the role that schools might play in affecting identity possibilities for interracial students. Might the interracial child go from being categorized on the basis of one race to actually believing he or she is monoracial, or at least appears to officially believe it? If the schools' categorization procedures frame the possibilities for how interracial children see themselves, the perceptions of interracial students would not just be tied to those particular situations, but most would extend beyond the particular context in which the situation is framed.

What other "cues" might this interracial child receive from the schools about how to identify himself or herself racially? If the primary function of the language of racial categorization is to direct social practice in the schools, then the production of compatible aspects of materials culture (e.g., curricula, books, cultural programs, class discussions) would be wholly integrated with it. But if the racial categorization procedures are merely a game to be overlooked ("to satisfy the government," as some would oversimplify), then there would be no connection to any other educational or social practices in the schools.

Central in my attempt in this book was to investigate the schools as influential sites for fostering or obstructing positive ethnic identity in interracial students. Since how the schools and the community classify interracial children might affect teachers' perceptions, such viewpoints bear with them the potential of affecting the racial self-image of multiracial students. Could teachers themselves, in addition to interracial students, internalize these instruments of categorization and thus unconsciously become agents of transmitting confused identities to interracial students based on mistaken policies?

Through the perceptions of teachers, I wanted to investigate the school environment that could control the web of racial possibilities for the interracial child. After I had investigated the written language by which interracial students are categorized, I wanted to examine teacher perceptions of those instruments and other "hidden curricula" in the school that would produce, legitimate, and transmit these written possibilities into other aspects of school material culture, so that those racial possibilities were maintained by everyone in the schools. If there were a web of specific instances in the schools that could tie the interracial student to monoracial possibilities, then a summary of all these events would make a monoracial identity plausible for the multiracial child.

URBAN VERSUS SUBURBAN

I interviewed 30 public school teachers from two towns in Massachusetts, one urban (U) and one suburban (S). Besides their urban/suburban difference, varying socioeconomic levels, and the varying number of multiracial children that "appear to be" in their district, there is also the public perception that the more urban city would be more sensitive to the issues and have more programs in place than the suburban schools. Although valid statistics cannot be available about the number of multiracial individuals in our schools due to our categorization procedures, it was felt that a more urban environment would have a larger number of multiracial families since it has a larger percentage per school of minorities. Also, most of the members of the Multiracial Family Network I directed were from the urban town and indicated a need for this study and offered support (which did become essential as I will note later). For the same reason, the smaller minority and possibly smaller multiracial population might prove to be a significant factor in affecting teacher awareness or resources and materials available in a given school system. A statistical comparison between the two towns compiled from the Individual School Report is shown in Table 1.

Upon reviewing the statistics in Table 1 it is clear that both towns are increasing their minority populations in the schools. In fact, in the urban environment minority school children are the majority population. Both towns also show significant increases among their Asian students, especially the suburban town that shows a decrease in enrollment for other minority groups. But one must wonder whether a significant portion of the urban town's 58.7 percent total minority population is actually multiracial? What percentage of the suburban town's 17.3 percent total minority is multiracial? Where do multiracial children fit in all this social algebra? Also, because the urban town's total minority population is the majority, which is about three times the number calculated for total minority in the suburban town, does this mean that the resources and awareness for multiracial school children should be much greater in the urban environment?

Permission was granted by the administrators of both school systems in February of 1991 for me to begin my research. However, my interviews with teachers did not begin until March of the following year. Initially, I experienced a great deal of difficulty in finding teachers to participate in the research when

Table 1
School Enrollment by Race

	1990	1996
URBAN TOWN		
Minority Total	53.1%	58.7%
White	46.9%	41.3%
Amer. Ind.	.1%	.4%
Black (not Hisp.)	32.7%	34.3%
Asian	6.6%	9.5%
Hispanic (non-white)	3.2% and 10.5% (white)	14.5%
SUBUBAN TOWN		
Minority Total	15.4%	17.3%
White	84.6%	82.7%
Amer. Ind.		.1%
Black (not Hisp.)	6.8%	5.8%
Asian	6.9%	9.1%
Hispanic (non-white)	.3% and 1.5% (white)	2.4%

Source: Based on the Bureau of Data Collection of the Massachusetts Department of Education, October 1, 1990 and 1996.

I solicited their assistance in traditional ways, for example, through letters in their school mailboxes. Although it could be concluded from this experience that they were either uncooperative or uncomfortable, I believe that the real reason is that teachers are very busy and probably have received little feedback or information about the research in which they participated in the past.

When addressed personally, whether on the playground during recess or through personal connections or just in the halls or libraries, teachers were extremely willing to be interviewed and continued to be supportive. In fact, most expressed a need to receive more information about the topic and I asked them questions that they had never thought about before. I never felt any lack of support in either school system.

One problem existed in the urban school system after I had completed interviews in the elementary schools and sought assistance to initiate my research at the town's high school. I was told that I had to get permission again, this time from the School

Senate, which meets monthly. I made many telephone calls, sent letters, and after a few months I was denied permission.

Since I already had permission from the town's Central Office administrators, as indicated in a letter, and had completed my research in the elementary schools, I was especially concerned since I felt research at the high school level was crucial to my project. I asked for my research to be reconsidered. I called parents of multiracial high school students who were part of the multiracial community group I founded and directed. These parents called the principal about my research and another date was set to review my proposal. I was allowed to personally address the group and permission was granted.

I can only guess why I met with such difficulties. It disturbed me especially since it happened in the town that was perceived as having a higher percentage of interracial children. I was told that the teachers were too busy, that there were a number of things that needed to be done and that my research maybe was not a priority. I am not sure if there was a valid reason why permission was denied, but I did lose a great deal of time.

In the suburban town, I also had a difficult time getting started. I received permission from an administrator of the Central Office who in turn said that the administrators would introduce my research to the principals. I was then told that there was no teacher response because it was the end of year. So I waited until September and I called the principals myself. Although I was told by the same school administrator that I couldn't contact principals independently, I felt that I could have friends address their principals and teachers on their own. I eventually was able to interview 15 teachers in both towns. What I learned most was that principals and teachers needed to be contacted personally and then they were very supportive for the most part. The standard official procedures took a great deal of time to implement and brought little support. While I had received the official permission required, some administrators, particularly those working in central offices and not working directly with students, did make it difficult to actually conduct the research.

A most alarming situation occurred when I called the suburban public school to check on the status of my research proposal. I waited a number of months and was anxious to commence my interviews. When I called the secretary, she responded, "I don't think it's here. I think that it was sent to Special Education." However, I was never able to verify if it was sent there or if the secretary was speaking on her own. In any event, her remark suggests how the average American might think about interracial children and under what "category" we might look as to where they might be serviced. This situation was particularly meaningful to me since I was a special educator for about ten years. In fact, I entered a Masters of Special Education program because I was told in the early 1970s while I was working in a culturally diverse community that I should pursue this area in order to service the "culturally deprived."

In an attempt to understand these difficulties in gaining assistance, I felt that a variety of reasons were plausible. First, teachers are very busy and are asked to contribute a great deal of time to research that they never hear about again. Second, at a time when there is considerable pressure in the schools to be "politically correct," a questionnaire about the status of interracial children is a threatening topic, especially for administrators.

TEACHER SELF-IDENTIFICATION

The semi-structured interview questions were divided into four sections of questions about the teachers and their perceptions: 1) biographical and educational background, 2) teacher and student reactions to school forms, 3) school material culture (e.g., curricula, materials, literature, and programs), and 4) teacher perceptions of multiracial children and the overall effects of racial categorization procedures on racial identity.

Most of the teachers interviewed were born and raised in New England and attended local colleges in Boston, except for four who were from other areas: Ohio, North Carolina, California, and Louisiana. When asked to define their race, all identified themselves as White, except for two, who self-defined as Asian American (Japanese and Chinese) and seven, who self-identified as Afro-American. Two teachers were married in-

terracially; one Caucasian female to a Jamaican and one
Afro-American to a Caucasian. Another teacher was the adop-
tive mother of an interracial child whom she described as phys-
ically and officially Black but culturally White. Another teacher
also taught a course in multicultural education at the graduate
school level in Boston.

I did not expect the following question to reveal more than
"just facts":

> *Q.* I am from————(country) and refer to myself as being
> of————(racial/ethnic) background.

What I found significant was a contradiction in how three
teachers self-defined their race in the beginning of the interview (Afro-American) and in how they later told me as "a matter of fact" that they were racially mixed. This switch to and
omission of a multiracial status during or after the interview
could possibly suggest some complex dynamics in multiracial
identity development and resolution.

I felt that this might reflect how interracial children might
be controlled by the official language of their identity and how
such obstacles might be unlatched from their perceptions. Most
Black Americans are multiracial, yet they have learned to identify monoracially as Black for complex sociopolitical reasons
that have been reinforced by the tools of our racial categorization system. The immediate teacher responses to questions
about their identity took on the form of society's official or familiar language, indicating that they identified as they were
taught to identify. This contradiction between the official language of their identity verses their actual and also perhaps suppressed identity illustrates the pressures that interracial
children might feel when they are trying to resolve this dilemma. Perhaps only in the course of the interview, which addressed the status of the interracial child in the school, did the
teachers feel that they did not have to choose loyalties between
the majority and minority race and that other choices might be
equally respectable.

Could this aid us in understanding what cultural cues might
be necessary for an interracial child to uncover and reconstitute

his or her suppressed multiracial identities? I began to see these teachers as evidence of how the system worked, for they had internalized these categories and were already victims of how our society thinks about race. However, they were not only positioned into sanctioned meanings for what their racial identity might be; they actively constructed meaning by analyzing the events in their everyday lives and conformed and perpetuated their practices as evidenced by their immediate responses to direct questions. Yet, by questioning the potential for other identity possibilities during the interview, was I sanctioning them as well and thus enabling them to analyze the events in their everyday lives? Was I, through the interview process, offering another format for a language of identification for interracial children, one that might position them within the realms of identifying with more than one race?

TEACHER AND STUDENT REACTIONS TO SCHOOL FORMS

As evidenced by our chapter on school forms, both towns have school registration forms, testing, and a number of opportunities to witness the racial categorization process. On the elementary level, all registration forms were filled out by parents; students were periodically asked to self-identify on state mandated tests at various other times. One teacher also told me that she takes racial attendance on a daily basis, while another showed me statistics on her minority special needs students. At the high school level, students were categorized racially in both towns. In town "U," racial categorization is also used to racially balance elementary schools as a volunteer solution rather than having to resort to forced busing. And at the high school level, racial categorizations were used to balance "houses" (units or smaller groupings of students designed so that students do not feel "lost" in larger schools). Might interracial students be used to "balance the racial books" by institutions themselves?

Q. Have you ever been surprised how a parent of an interracial child has categorized their child?

Several teachers in town "U" on the elementary level reported being surprised about how the parents of interracial children had reported their children racially. Most noted that parents often chose to report the race that was "most needed" to racially balance the schools. This was especially true of Black/White children whose parents chose White because that would ensure their entrance into certain "good" or neighborhood schools that have a higher minority ratio. This became especially crucial in schools that had bilingual programs for Haitians and other linguistic minorities who would upset or tip the majority/minority balance.

One interracial elementary student in the urban school recalled that her parents checked off both races before they were called by the school and later changed her race to White. This student saw it as part of a game she played but that she really saw herself as both Black and White. Another teacher spoke about a Cape Verdean child whose mother insisted her daughter was White, only to switch later when she found the school across the street needed more Blacks. In another case, a biracial child whose mother and stepfather were White, identified their child as White because they wanted their child to identify with them as parents, for example, "You're White like Mom and Dad."

The absurdity of forcing children of multiple heritage to identify with only one race forces that same system to be inconsistent in its reporting. A teacher told me about a light-skinned Cape Verdean woman who was married to a Black American and whose children were identified in the hospital by the doctor as Black if the father was present at the birth and White if he wasn't. Hence, some of her lighter skinned children are "Black" and some of her dark skinned children are "White." Another teacher told me that it was possible in the earlier days of eyeballing students that siblings were initially sent to different schools because their races appeared to be different.

Such inconsistencies can serve as powerful tools for affecting government funding allocated to towns to service minority students. Multiracial children become part of "racial politics" whereby their codification can be itemized and juggled from one group to another. Special programs, tutors, books, counselors, and other resources and materials available for minority students are dependent, in part, on the inclusion of multiracial students in their numbers. One is overwhelmed by numbers and percentages when looking at the Individual School Report, and after interviewing teachers one can only guess the part that racially mixed children could play in this process. Imagine such statements as: "We need more Whites here in this district." "There aren't enough Asian kids for this project." "This foundation wants to help Hispanic kids." "We need more minority teachers in proportion to our students."

Such codifications are largely responsible for keeping multiracial students "minority" in all aspects of school culture. Multiracial students unknowingly are pawns in the numbers game of the political organizational structures that influence school policy and govern student-teacher interaction. Whatever race the multiracial child or school personnel ultimately chooses "to go with" on an official school form is rooted in some organizational aspect of the official curriculum and ultimately becomes its hidden curriculum. Multiracial students often unknowingly accept being pawns and reinforce the practice through their own participation in its entitlement programs.

> *Q.* Can you describe to me one instance in which you remember having to racially categorize an interracial student or an instance when an interracial student was categorizing himself/herself?

When teachers were asked whether they have seen students struggling with their identity, particularly when filling out school racial categorization questions, various stories emerged around themes of identity (confusion, resolution; definition of identity terms and redefinition of terms). In most cases, the race "of choice" was based not on how the child might have felt but what monoracial categorization was advantageous to the child at any particular moment. Such situational pressures institutionalized the forcing and/or suppression of racial identities in interracial children. Note the following teachers' observations:

> *A.* Some say, "I can't answer that question, it has no meaning to me. Where we come from it has no connection to

anything. . . . You decide." And I answer "I can't register you unless you pick one of the six categories, even though I may totally agree with you, even from what you are saying to me or from what I'm interpreting from your expressions." . . . May or may not be a biracial situation in the home. Then when you have the obvious situation, when you see both parents and one is Black and one is White; whatever, usually that is what it is. And if the child is there it becomes a very difficult situation to pick one or the other. The bureaucracy wants some way to be able to categorize people for reporting purposes. . . . Not easy to do, if they refuse, I put down refuse to answer the question. . . . It's a silly thing. Kids seem the most pained, more than the parent. It's the kids who have to make a choice. . . . You see them shrug . . . you know.

A. I saw some disastrous eyeballing, especially when I taught a long time ago. I remember a situation where a teacher came in and said to light skinned Blacks, "For now you are all White" and the kids were in tears. They wanted the schools to be integrated and they needed more Whites.

A. Yes, I remember a girl who couldn't think of herself as Black and didn't want anyone to think of her as Black.

A. A girl was put into the Black category and said, "I am not Black American. I'm Cape Verdean." . . . Others said, "I'm Haitian Creole."

A. I had an interracial child who kept changing her name, who didn't have a clear idea of who she was, and I understand that she had done this since birth, hadn't had an idea of who she was. So if she wasn't happy with one thing, she would change and be another thing, and while that was just names, there was this whole piece of identity because she knew her father was Black and her mother was White and sometimes she just had confusion about what that made her. . . . Have seen students struggle with it, not know how to speak about it or [be] in denial of it. Young people are candid and say, "You don't look like this person. You don't look White. How can you call yourself White?" . . . On the basic skill test it is tricky and they do ask the kids, and sometimes the kids don't know and say I'm not sure, and I say let me look on your official form and see what your parents had to say about this issue. . . . Sometimes they say, "I'm not sure how I'm categorized. Am I Black? Am I White?" And I say, "Let me check. It could be either one." Sometimes if they don't want to deal with it, I say, "Leave it blank and I'll fill it in."

A. It usually depends upon the politics of the individual, rare for a child to identify as White, some both, most Black. . . . Most identify with the underdog.

When asked,

Q. What do you think about classifying students on the basis of race?

A. It raises racist feelings . . .

A. Government seems to need it. . . . I don't feel comfortable with it.

A. The first question is to ask why we need to categorize and if the answer is to better serve the population, by identifying distribution, density and impact, I would support it.

A. We can get used to negative things; if racial categorization will increase federal funding for minorities, then it is o.k.

Almost all teachers saw racial categorization as a procedure that had strong negative connotations because as many teachers stated, "It raises racist feelings." However, the consensus was that such procedures were tolerated as a "necessary evil" when you have a pluralistic society and the schools need to be racially balanced.

Q. If we must have racial categorization procedures, what is the best method?

Q. What about a separate category for students of more than one race?

When asked what would be the best way to categorize interracial students and if a separate category was desirable, most
said that they wished that they could check off all their races
and have them count rather than have a separate category. But
most assumed that would not happen and supported the idea
of a separate category. Most teachers transferred their negative
feelings about racial categorization procedures in general to
how they felt about another and separate category. For example,

A. Now you're setting up isolation. You're making a statement that there's something different about you, good or
bad.

A. No, more difficult.

The idea that equality entails ignoring differences (and thus
the cultural distinctiveness of multiracial children) is a popular
notion that provides the key as to why we need a separate category. Historically, interracial marriage and children have
been perceived in marginal ways; and thus it was "best not to
notice" their difference. However, this strategy has failed them.
Although the American public is most reverent about racial
equality, the concept of affirming and recognizing group difference is misunderstood as a contradiction of that reverence.
While the American people may herald the public declaration
"People are all the same" as their core value, it is less at the
heart of how they really feel. Young notes, "The achievement
of formal equality does not eliminate social differences, and
rhetorical commitment to the sameness of persons makes it impossible even to name how those differences presently structure
privilege and oppression" (1990: 164). The American system of
racial categorization is an example of one of the organizational
structures through which privilege and oppression are sanctioned. Interracial students' "differentness" needs to be noticed,
understood, and affirmed rather than ignored, misunderstood,
and negated in the schools because multiracial students are
invisible on all school forms.
Thus, although one benefit of the racial categorization proc-

ess is that it forces the recognition of minority groups and the allocation of funds for them, by confining the identity possibilities of multiracial students to one race in all its documentation, it possibly has institutionalized established patterns for the exclusion of our perceptions about interracial children and how we allocate resources for them.

We need to look at how this categorization documentation plays out in the classroom to determine whether or not the racial identity of interracial children is enhanced or inhibited in our school culture. With this in mind, we will turn to how teachers view the school environment, which helps frame identity possibilities for these children. Does monoracial documentation translate into teacher perceptions, resources, materials, and the rest of school culture, thus putting sociopolitical pressures upon the multiracial child? Could something as technical as the "one category" procedure become an ideological framework from which interracial children idealize how they see themselves racially?

SCHOOL CULTURE

What other artifacts of cultural formation besides school documentation provide a basis for interracial children to discover the possible identities for themselves in the schools? If one of the "hidden curricula" of our current racial categorization system in the schools is to "steer and direct social practice" toward monoracial destinies, then the schools' production of compatible aspects of material culture (i.e., books, curricula, cultural programs, class discussions, rituals) is wholly integrated into it.

According to Giroux, people individually learn to invest both intellectually and emotionally in particular ideologies and social practices by conforming to the everyday events in their lives. In this way, the dynamics of everyday life is linked to the political ideologies of the dominant culture. Mary Douglas emphasizes how these everyday events that frame how each individual thinks and feels are controlled by that which has been sanctioned by others of their social grouping, whether it be directly through a parent, family, or organization, or indirectly through their instruments of control, such as rules, rituals, ceremonies, or other cultural artifacts. The only important ingredient is that the group is authorized and therefore has the power to control private thought without our knowing that we are even surrendering control. The schools are social as well as educational institutions that are licensed by us to encode information, make routine decisions, and solve routine problems even about our social well being. In fact, they do "a lot of regular thinking on behalf of individuals" (1986: 47).

The schools as an institution of the dominant culture have the power to control racial possibilities for the multiracial child through their implementation of a racial categorization system and other supportive cultural forms (curricula, resources, cultural programming, rituals). These contextual clues influence the perceptions of the multiracial child as part of a wider "accumulation of collective memories and stories, that provide students with a sense of familiarity, identity and practical knowledge" (Giroux 1989: 146). In fact, possibly more culture is transmitted through this "hidden curriculum" than through the school's formal curriculum.

If we alter our monoracial categorization structure by adding a multiracial category, will we also alter our monoracial perceptions of mixed race students and improve the situations and experiences for them? Will the schools' "hidden curricula" remain the same or will they immediately adapt to new terminology? Have students already questioned our racial social order or accepted it as an unquestioned truth? If they have questioned it, why have they not been changed? If they have not questioned the racial social order, why and how has this particular aspect of our collective culture—that is, a monoracial classification for all children—been presented in school as objective, factual knowledge?

Teachers and parents may be unaware of what we are actually teaching our children about race, tenets that might jeopardize the happiness of the multiracial child. With this in mind, we will attempt to uncover a more complete picture of how multiracial children formulate racial perceptions of themselves by analyzing what teachers perceive is reflected for them in their curricula, books, cultural programs, class discussions, and other forms of cultural transformations. However, first we need

to know what is given to teachers to prepare them to teach
interracial children.

Q. Did you receive information about interracial children
in your teacher training?

The teachers' biographical and educational backgrounds suggest that teachers' informal training through their everyday
experiences either living or working among multiracial populations was a key factor in determining their level of awareness.
For example, teachers from California and Louisiana and those
who taught in urban situations seemed to be more familiar with
the topic and had more stories to tell. However, neither of these
factors influenced their formal teacher training or the resources
available in their schools. Not one teacher remembered receiv-
ing any information about interracial children in their teacher
training.

Class Discussions

Q. Can you think of any time in which the issue of racial
identity is raised in the classroom or in any other way?
When does it come up?

The issue of racial identity, while not seemingly part of any
formal curriculum, did surface occasionally in informal discussions in the classroom. In fact, the three teachers who said it
was discussed were vague about specific instances and often
drew upon negative instances. One related the issue to her subject matter ("for example, in history or literature"), while another related it to a negative experience ("You see it when they
strike out in anger, for example, 'your mother's Black' . . . even
though they could be the best of friends"). Another teacher reported feeling very uncomfortable when a young boy said, "I
don't want to marry a Black woman when I grow up" in the
presence of a biracial girl. When asked "why not" by the
teacher, the boy responded, "because some of my children might
be Black."

Q. Suppose a teacher knew she had an interracial child in the class and suppose that teacher also discussed multicultural issues with her class, would you be likely to talk about people of more than one race?

The majority of teachers concurred that most teachers would talk only in monoracial terms and that it would not occur to them to include multiracial populations without the subject surfacing on its own. For example, "when we talk about family, looking at biographies and family trees" or "when discussing civil rights, melting pot, affirmative issues," the topic might surface. Others mentioned various instances in which it might have been relevant in history and English classes but were not able to give a complete picture of a typical conversation. Those who said, "sure" or "I think so" could not give instances when this would occur. This question also made some teachers uncomfortable.

It was very clear that there was little recognition of the multiracial child in the classroom. In fact, since a few teachers erroneously suggested some "good books about multiracial children" that were actually books about multiracial children identifying monoracially and never multiracially suggests that a number of teachers still "do not get it" and would not be capable of transmitting a multiracial identity in the classroom. Even though the same teachers may have had a clear sense of definition of the "multiracial" child ("of more than one race"), this knowledge did not appear to shape their beliefs or practices in the classroom.

I felt that most teachers innocently transferred monoracial minority messages to multiracial children. When this possibility was addressed, most of the teachers agreed and felt badly about it. One teacher responded, "we give the same signals to multiracial students that we give for students of all races, there are no clear messages for them. I'm sure that there is a lot of confusion about how to feel. I'm sure that there are questions popping in their heads."

Cultural Programs

Q. Suppose the school had a day to celebrate cultural differences. Would the school be likely to have a program about being multiracial?

Cultural programming as a form of popular culture is viewed as an "extra" curriculum in the schools; it does not have the status of the formal curriculum of classroom studies. Nonetheless, it is especially significant in shaping how the school population "ought" to think about issues and what art forms are "new" and "fun" and thus important to know. It introduces new ideas and expresses old and valuable ones. What gets programmed or not programmed is a selective process. Thus, by choosing to produce certain cultural events and/or issues and ignoring others, the school grants a certain amount of credibility and importance to some ideas and not to others. Furthermore, it is important to look very closely at *how* the event is presented. Is there anything that might bear a hidden agenda, or is there an assumption that all facets of the issue are included when there may be an issue that has been ignored? What gets ignored and what doesn't is important to know. The schools need to take another look at what may be viewed as trivial as part of the schools' "hidden curriculum," which has a very powerful effect on shaping how students think and determining what is the appropriate way to express themselves culturally.

Both schools had multicultural celebrations and specific cultural events. Hence, we can say that multiculturalism is important in the schools. School "S" had a series "Growing Up Afro-American," "Growing Up Italian-American," "Growing up Asian-American," but never was there any separate recognition or inclusion of any multicultural programming for the multiracial child. I thought about all the interracial students who might find a sanctioned group to identify with in clubs for Black, Asian, or Hispanic students through which they could participate and continue to affirm their monoracial status.

Most often participation in these social groups assumes that one affirms only the stated piece of racial identity.

However, an interesting situation occurred at a Martin Luther King Day assembly at the urban high school. A foreign student came forward on a stage facing 600 of her peers and said that she was proud to be of mixed origin. The counselor who related this story to me seemed to be very familiar and sensitive to this issue, a fact that she attributed to her life in New Orleans, where racial mixture is more common and acknowledged. She felt that for any Black/White student listening this was a "unique and incredible" experience.

Curriculum

Q. Could you suggest any strategies or materials that might be effective in helping teachers reinforce a positive racial identity in interracial children?

When asked about whether they were aware of any specific curriculum, teacher resources, or materials, most said there weren't any and those who said there were, were confusing such materials with curricula and resources for minority students. Racially mixed individuals are absent in all school curricula, including in history and English texts. Yet, many noted minority role models are actually interracial. This difference is never noted. Although I checked for teacher resources on this topic, I did not find any. However, I am not aware that any resources exist at all that might guide the teacher to best serve interracial students. Nor did I find that interracial children had any clear visibility in current multicultural education resources. However, I believe there is a general assumption on the part of educators that "surely there must be."

Books

I checked most school libraries in both towns and in only two incidents were teachers aware of specific books in their schools. One teacher who is the parent of a multiracial child said, "Everyone drags out their one book of *Black Is Brown Is Tan*." In the other incident, there was another book mentioned that included multiracial messages as part of the positive messages given to children. However, no other teacher in that school was aware that the book existed.

Two teachers were anxious to show me books they had about interracial children. However, when I asked to see them, it was clear that once again the books fostered positive monoracial "black" identities in interracial children. One book entitled *Colors Like Me* showed children with different skin shades of black on each page, yet the children belonged in the Black culture ("Mary is like the color of a peach . . . John is like a chocolate cake"). Although it is a beautiful book, the message is quite clear. It is a book for interracial children of various skin shades, hair textures, and other physical features that promotes identifying monoracially as Black. While it is important that this book be available to those children who choose this option, it was scary that not even their teachers understood (at least not until I pointed it out) that this book was another example of how the schools might control how interracial children perceive themselves racially.

Most teachers, like the librarians previously mentioned, had assumed that such books were readily available and once again confused this issue with books for monoracial minority children. Most felt shocked and somewhat betrayed that there weren't any such books in their schools. Some were very protective of their schools and insisted that the school must have them but still only one teacher knew of any.

Thus, according to teachers and other school personnel, the resources and materials that do exist for interracial children are not available in the schools. Furthermore, it was assumed that such information constitutes the same resources as that pertaining to all minority children. In fact, one teacher, who later admitted that he is mixed, showed me the pictures of famous "model Black Americans" (who he claimed were actually racially mixed people) that he uses for discussions. Most teachers needed to have the unique situation of interracial children explained to them. For example, in the case of the school librarian who was certain that his urban school had had such books since the sixties, when I restated my request and clarified the difference between books for minority children, he said, "Oh, well, we wouldn't have those books here in the students' library. They'd be upstairs with the teacher resources." Of course, there was no information there either.

It is important to note how this lack in importance of reinforcing multiracial identity is part of a wider problem that exists in the community. When I first visited the central library of the suburban town, there were no books for or about multiracial children. After using every conceivable "key word" to get information, I approached the children's librarian who was confident that they had such books and she proudly showed me a stack of monoracial minority books. Again, I had to explain what I was looking for. She was so insistent that there must be some mistake. As I left, I saw her huddling over her computer. Could she be searching for that special key word that would prove me wrong?

Just before this book was printed, I rechecked this same library in order to compose a list of multiracial children's books as a resource for this book (see Further Reading). I was given the 1997 *Books in Print* and other resource books, including multicultural ones, and had an impossible time accessing information using a multitude of key words to describe multiracial children (incidentially, the word "multiracial" does not exist in the library). I was also given a list of over 40 books entitled "Inter-Racial Friends & Families" of which less than 10 were about multiracial children rather than friendships. Checking all of the resources available in the library, my personal collection of articles in interracial family newsletters, and book companies that specialize in multicultural books, I was able to compose my list. However, I constantly had to delete entries because many of these books were out of print. Since the market for these books is small, even recently published books will go out of print. I could not imagine how difficult it would be for the multiracial child to access such books for their own use, especially since many multiracial children would feel uncomfortable asking for assistance.

In the suburban newspaper, a story was reported about a new multicultural book business that had books about children from 18 different ethnic/racial groups. The article listed all eighteen groups in an obvious attempt to be inclusive of all groups in the town regardless of its small population. Yet, books about racially mixed children were not included in the list. Such incidents illustrate that deliberate measures need to be taken by parents of multiracial children in order to prevent such omissions from continuing to happen. Multiracial individuals deserve the same automatic recognition and inclusion as all children in their schools, libraries, and neighborhoods.

TEACHER PERCEPTIONS

Q. What effect, if any, might racial categorization procedures on the basis of one race have on how teachers perceive interracial students?

Teachers did not respond immediately to the question. Although they were aware of the power their perspectives might have on how all students feel about their self-image, they were not aware that they too could be affected by these procedures and transfer their thoughts to their students.

Teachers play a vital role in influencing how children think about themselves. They bring into the classroom their perceptions, which act as a form of legitimation for influencing their students beyond the classroom. In this way, teachers have the authority to affirm or reject the social ordering of the schools as an institution that transmits identity possibilities to them. Are teachers aware of the control they have over their students' perceptions and more importantly, are they aware of the control they have over their own? Teacher-student interactions are governed by the organizational structures of the schools' hidden curricula whose values shape almost every aspect of student life.

Q. What does the term "interracial" mean to you?

Q. How many interracial children are you teaching this year, last year?

Although most teachers reported a clear sense of definition of an interracial child ("two or more races"), all around them were contradictions that would confuse or obstruct these definitions, so that multiracial possibilities were least likely to be transmitted through teacher reinforcement. Also, in a few cases teachers confused interracial with intercultural. A few teachers explained the term properly as being children of racial mixture, only to identify in their class as interracial those students whose parents were from different countries, but not different races.

This made me think about how important the issue of race is in comparison to the issue of ethnicity. To a much greater extent than ethnicity, race, in most cases, has visible borders that are bolstered by inflexible sociopolitical constructs. Unlike White Americans of mixed ethnic intermarriages who are personally selecting their identities from the several available to them (Waters 1990), children of mixed race are more likely to have their identities predetermined by a society that confines them to only one. No one questions multiethnic identity but multiracial identity is problematic both socially and institutionally.

How teachers perceived this monoracial process of identification in the schools—the "why" and "how" and "if" interracial students should be categorized—is related to how the teachers formulated their perceptions about race and is ultimately connected to how multiracial children come to accept the status quo of a nation that marginalizes individuals.

> *Q.* If a teacher had to fill out a form in which he or she had to classify an interracial child on the basis of one race, what would the teacher be likely to base the decision on? What is most important? Least important? Facial characteristics, skin color, spoken language, minority race, majority race, surname?

When asked how interracial children might be categorized under current monoracial restrictions by teachers themselves, if they had to make those decisions, most teachers felt uncomfortable, and some refused to answer. But a majority agreed and though initially seemed to accept this line of questioning as "sort of a game" they would play, they took it very seriously.

Most said something similar to "everyone categorizes on the basis of skin color for it's the easiest way to identify race"; but a few were aware of the contradictions in this basis for racial identification (e.g., "Skin color is last because it is tricky.") What was also interesting about this question is that the teachers' answers revealed that most people think of the Black/White racial mixture when referring to interracial students. However, when questions were posed about children of specific racial unions, more detailed stories surfaced.

Q. What about interracial Black/White children?

A. Black/White children would be categorized on the basis of whatever he or she phenotypically looks like. In a situation where you can't decide and know of children who don't look Black, the guilt of denying part of yourself is troubling. It is tough on some who are phenotypically White and must identify as Black.

A. I usually depend upon the politics of the individual. It's rare for a child to identify as White. Some identify as both. Most identify as Black.

When discussing identity categorizations of other racial mixtures, variables other than skin color (e.g., surname and spoken language) that would influence how to identify these children were mentioned. What was significant was that despite where one got cues about a student's minority status, it was clear that children of all racial mixtures were to be categorized as minorities. Thus, the task seemed to be not to determine if they would be this race or that race but what was the "key" that would unlatch this minority identity.

Q. What about Amerasian children?

Although some teachers mentioned that some Amerasian students might not look Asian or have an Asian surname and that some of these students might be identified as White, the "correct" choice would be minority if it were discovered. I immediately thought of a teacher I interviewed who failed to mention that she had any Amerasian students even when I specifically asked her if she did. Since she was a teacher of some Amerasian students I know, whose White mother had actually requested the interview for me, I was surprised. Then I realized that she had never met the father of these students, who also has a very distinct Chinese surname.

Q. What about interracial Hispanic students?

When the teachers discussed the racial identity of interracial Hispanic students, their main clue seemed to be whether or not the child spoke Spanish in the home. Although this might give a clue, most said that since some Hispanics are White, that the visual clues were confusing and that they would only know very superficially whether a student was a racial or ethnic minority. A few teachers acknowledged some foreign students from Latin America or Portugal whom they did not know what to do about when it came to racial categorization. This signaled to me a need for clarification between race and culture (i.e., the reliance on linguistic clues especially when considering Hispanic students).

Q. What if the child is of two minority races?

When asked about students who were comprised of at least two minority mixtures, the dilemma became more complicated. It seemed that in these cases, as it should have been in the others, making a decision was much more difficult and in the words of one teacher was "a political football," as shown in the following examples:

A. I have a student who has a Puerto Rican mother and Black father and she is classified as Hispanic, and I think I'd do the same thing if there is Spanish spoken at home and if there is some identification with being of Spanish heritage also.

A. The issue of categorizing children of two different minority races does come up when students self-select.

Which one did I feel most represented their race? I was probably inconsistent in how I dealt with it, I probably based it on appearance if the child was Black and Hispanic. However, if the Hispanic side was strong—for example, if English was their second language—then I surmised that the Hispanic side was more predominant than Black. However, there are a number of countries that speak Spanish too and selecting one race seems impossible.

A. Black, because we are documenting them for a special project to raise Black achievement.

A. In the case of Afro-Asian students, most say Black to identify with the underdog.

Thus, how the world comes to see and categorize interracial children is a process filled with illogical and inconsistent ideas that are not meant to work as long as the system of reference is monoracial. Choosing one race when one is of more than one race could only be illogical. Politics controls how mixed race children are perceived rather than validating how they might feel. Since the greatest polarization that exists is between Black and White culture, even one drop of Black blood, whether visible or not, seems to be the "sanctioned choice." In fact, this seems to be the same answer when considering all racial mixtures in which Caucasian is one race. The White identity is suppressed. When considering children who are of two minority races, it seems that other variables are considered equally, making the decision more complicated. However, in the final analysis, choosing the Black identity predominates in these decisions. As one teacher claimed, "loyalty to the underdog" is an important factor. This was an interesting idea because the word "underdog" validates a response to a social order that is superimposed by the "overdogs" of society.

Ironically, the "one drop only" rule that was created as a necessary tool of dominance by the White culture to separate Whites from "others," "subordinates," and "underdogs" is still being culturally constructed under the guise of "protecting the underdogs." The very fact that the minority races reinforce this

White rule of dominance is viewed by researchers in different ways. On the one hand, there is the viewpoint that this tool of dominance illustrates how minority groups buy into the system of racial domination by demanding that any attachment to the White race be extinguished. "Recent pride in being a person of color has demanded full-fledged commitment to the racial and ethnic minority group in order to pass 'legitimacy tests' " (Root 1992: 8). How interracial teachers themselves responded indicates that they passed the test.

But there is another dimension to how this action is viewed. Some convincingly argue that turning symbols and practices like this upside down is a common resistance strategy (Lincoln 1989). In this sense, showing "loyalty to the underdog" would become a strategy of empowerment. By showing loyalty and bonding with their group, giving them additional strength, minority groups take the initiative to restructure how we experience the word "underdog" so that it becomes a symbol of power and resistance rather than of control by White society.

Thus, the process of categorizing students was especially problematic for teachers who are in an atmosphere in which the social understanding of race has allowed only one category. "Unfortunately this problematic taxonomy has been transformed into a sociopolitical system that has been imprinted in our psyches. Subsequently, race has become enmeshed with our social structure, determining the distribution of resources among social groups" (Root 1992: 8). Even though by definition interracial children are of more than one race, they suffer under the monoracial reality of how they are categorized and ultimately perceived.

I found that most teachers had a basic understanding about the identity issues of interracial students but that teachers in the urban environment, having more exposure to the topic, had much more detailed information. Most emphasized that adolescence might be a particularly crucial time for mixed race students, not so much because of internal struggles that need to be worked out, but because of socioeconomic and political constraints in relationships that surface during this period.

Q. Can you think of a particular time when the interracial child is more likely to experience greater difficulty about his racial identity?

A. Middle school is when the issue of racial identity begins to appear as an issue. Younger children interact interracially but around middle school they separate into racial groups. Where do biracial kids sit? They sit in both places, not moving back and forth; the poor kids hang out with Black kids while the richer kids hang out with White kids. Where one lives and goes to church is important, whether or not they are in Black or White communities.

A. It is hard for those who are dating. They are forced to make a choice about who they are and who they're going to hang out with.

A. Adolescents wrestle with it in dating, not in elementary school but in junior high and high school. Kids separate into groups and they sort out, especially the upper middle-class kids who associate with middle-class Whites.

A. It is at this time that interracial students start to go "very street," meaning that they have to compensate for being Black by over-illustrating Blackness.

Thus, it appears that it is at this time that interracial students are forced to decide (or have the community decide for them) which group they will formally identify as their race. According to the testimony of some of the teachers, where one lives—whether in a Black, White, or integrated neighborhood—is a factor in determining with whom one is most comfortable identifying. Yet, interracial Black/White students must also weigh additional pressures to identify with the street culture of "being Black."

Teachers also revealed how the different races are perceived by the children. One third grade teacher stated, "I have two: Spanish/Black and White/Afro-American who tend to be with Black groups, but that doesn't mean they don't have other friends. If there is hostility, they drop back on race by making such comments such as, 'Just because you're White, you think you're better than we are.' Several years ago I heard, 'You're picking on me because I am Black but my mother's White and she's gonna come and get you.' " This statement revealed how the different races are perceived by the children.

Had teachers internalized these stereotypes about monoracial groups so that categorization procedures might have had an effect on how they perceive interracial children? According to one teacher who is a parent of a multiracial child, "Teachers who already have preconceived notions will lump together the interracial child with notions pertinent to that one race." When asked:

Q. What affect, if any, might racial categorization procedures on the basis of race have on how teachers perceive interracial students?

A. Some teachers view interracial children more favorably than Black children.

A. It affects how one might push you in school. If students look Asian, teachers might push them more.

While it was clear that teachers might delegate certain monoracial stereotypes to multiracial children, most teachers do not understand how such categorizations would be related to the wider picture of how we have come to process race in a singular, fixed way.

Almost all the teachers interviewed were aware of the difficulties of interracial students and pleased to talk to someone about their needs. Most felt that the issue of multiracial identity was discussed in the classroom only "if it came up" in the context of other issues that had a racial theme, for example, in a history or English class or during a racially explosive incident. Even then the issues of multiple identity for interracial children were almost never reinforced, and most felt that both teachers and students needed a more balanced perspective. My conversations with teachers seemed to make most of them aware of all the monoracial cues that the education system reinforced and that cues that supported multiracial identity options were practically non-existent. With few exceptions, teachers felt that interracial children needed instruction so that more inclusive options about their identity could be presented to them. When asked what was necessary to bring about this cultural transformation in the schools, a variety of responses revealed the need to create new materials and revise old materials because existent materials did not reinforce this identity option. They mentioned books, curricula, films, cultural programs, clubs, and discussions.

However, most were aware that in order for these materials to have a lasting effect, teacher training, discussions, and public dialogues need to take place so that all identity options could be presented to students, teachers, and the community. Through these means, interracial students, their teachers, and their families would be able to make a more informed choice. One teacher suggested that teachers reexamine their own identity and "go back to fine tune their own sense of who they are. White teachers need to be reminded that they also have a culture; everyone needs to affirm their own heritage. When teachers are able to do that for themselves, then they can do that kind of work for their students. Many biracial children have been locked out of their White European heritage."

Despite these discussions, toward the end of the interview a number of teachers revealed that having a strong Black identity was more important. "It [having multiracial options presented to the students for a more informed choice] is important, but [the biracial students] must have a strong Black identity. . . . That is how society sees them." This fallback position suggested to me that even though most teachers might be interested in reexamining the hidden, monoracial messages that interracial students receive in the schools, teachers were not necessarily ready to change the pattern of monoracial treatment of mixed race students. Their reluctance to take a stand on this issue was a warning to me that there might be difficulty for multiracial individuals to attain support should it appear that it would jeopardize minority power struggles. Teachers' defense of their position in support of a monoracial Black identity through such phrases as "how society sees them" trivializes the cause of multiracial students and masks a stronger conviction many teachers have to be "loyal to the underdog."

This is a complex issue. Our society has long seen interracial children of Black/White mixture as Black, which has been viewed in negative terms. Now, the notion of Black pride has taken hold as a strategy to resist White dominance and to unite Blacks with pride. This movement has included interracial children, who were encouraged to think, "Yes, we are Black and proud." However, currently many members of the multiracial community are seeking to do the same thing for their children. And one example of this is a call for a separate "multiracial" category. It too can be perceived as a call for resistance against the pressure to identify monoracially and as a call for pride and strength through unity, whereby interracial students are encouraged to think, "Yes, we're mixed or half-breeds and proud of it." There is again some shifting of racial identity roles for interracial children and the renegotiation with their communities as to how they will be perceived.

This issue needs to be re-examined by society, and the schools could serve an important role in spearheading this effort. Monoracial identity for interracial children has been widely understood as an appropriate description by the society that determines ultimately how they see themselves. If all interracial students are to feel more comfortable about their identity, including those who struggle with identifying monoracially, multiple identity options also need to be presented and supported through both the institutions and schools and their agents (i.e., teachers and school personnel who transmit identities). If the goal of education is to serve all children in our pluralistic society, then we are falling short of this goal by shortchanging mixed race children, by making them invisible in the schools in almost all aspects of cultural transformation.

The statement by Epps that begins this chapter illustrates one of the many ways in which our multicultural endeavors to acknowledge diversity have shut out interracial children. Could it actually be true that not even a tiny thought was given to them when a whole array of changes was made concerning mi-

nority cultures in the 1980s and 1990s? There is no evidence
that there was any consideration of their differences. "What
diversity do we silence in the name of a liberatory pedagogy?"
(Giroux 1988: xii). Throughout almost every aspect of our entire
educational system nationwide, from its formal curricula and
practices to its informal and hidden curricula and practices,
interracial children are omitted and thus do not exist. In fact,
perhaps *mono*cultural education rather than *multi*cultural education is the more appropriate term for what we are now
teaching in schools. But then, as I have suggested before, there
is no one-to-one correspondence between our language used and
the reality of the situation. The word "multicultural" is a sociopolitical construct that ought to be questioned, especially
when one considers how our multicultural education has fixed
cultural borders that have ignored multiracial children.

Now is the time to re-examine what multicultural education
lacks. Most educators are in favor of greater inclusion for our
diverse students and would be appalled at the omission of multiracial children. In fact, the notion of multicultural education
began with a degree of indignation about the lack of representation of varied cultures. School personnel, from teachers to
aids to principals to custodians, are well meaning and concerned about creating a just and multicultural society. But our
system of monoracial categorization has prevented school personnel and most of us from affirming the multiracial reality of
our multiracial students. This very technical and statistical
procedure is not only a symbol of how our nation thinks about
race, it is also a symptom that signals how we exclude multiracial students in our schools.

One insightful teacher clearly stated the reason for legitimizing more racial identity options for multiracial students. "I
think it is helpful if it helps children to begin to see themselves
more pluralistically. If you don't have to identify with one culture as being the best, then there are benefits and richness in
different cultures. If you have more than one culture, then you
are doubly blessed." Nevertheless, the statement "But society
sees them as of one race" illustrates how society has a sociopolitical dilemma that has caused pain for a number of mixed

race children. America should change how Americans continue to reinforce this notion of monorace, so that different cues will set off identity options that include the racially mixed child. Change can take place in an important way in the schools.

6

Inclusion: Making the Invisible Visible

> When someone with the authority of a teacher, say, describes the world and you are not in it, there is a moment of psychic disequilibrium, as if you looked into a mirror and saw nothing.
>
> —Adrienne Rich

Our nation's system of racial categorization has become a very strong symbol in the multiracial community because it is believed that monoracial categorization acts as a foundation for a much wider array of sociocultural experiences that define, legitimize, and transmit racial identities to mixed race children. My concern has been that the experiences that take place in schools might contribute to how interracial children see themselves racially. I was more than just interested, and I am now, as a result of my work, concerned that schools (and the rest of the American public) do unknowingly make the normal racial identity development process problematic for those students who might want to select more than one racial identity.

For years interracial organizations nationwide have tried to change racial categorization policies at both the local and federal levels. The first legislation requiring multiracial children to be allowed to identify multiracially in the schools was passed in 1992 in the state of Ohio, and many other groups of parents of interracial children are working with their local school boards to have multiracial identity options included on school forms. However, this alteration is more symbolic than significant since changes still need to be made on a federal level for the more accurate identities to show up on national statistical calculations. Nor do our government policies challenge classic norms; identity is not fixed but fluid—shifting and multiple. The schools, mandated to uphold these statistical procedures for tabulating race, treat difference as a technical rather than political category.

Rosaldo is worth quoting at length as his work on cultural visibility and invisibility is relevant to our subject:

> Seen from a distinct but related angle of vision, the conceptual difficulties that have created zones of relative cultural visibility and invisibility derive in large part from tacit methodological norms that conflate the notion of culture with the idea of difference. In this sense the term "cultural difference" is as redundant as that of "cultural order." (1993: 201)

By affirming only one of a person's racial identities, our racial categorization process has relegated interracial children to a curious kind of "hybrid invisibility" (Rosaldo 1993). Because of such cultural containment, interracial children are stymied in having a distinctive cultural identity.

In many ways, the interracial child is a microcosm of American cultural identity. The interracial child shares with his or her wider American community the difficulties of coping with its diverse heritage, but on a deeper, personal level. America in the 1990s is still in multicultural process, still renegotiating its own racial and ethnic identity—or dare I say identities—and interracial children bear the burden of these difficulties. The call for politically correct language is a response to these difficulties. Though political correctness is an important attempt to respect the distinctiveness of America's racial and ethnic groups, it has failed to acknowledge the multiracial child, possibly because America has not reached the point of recognizing similarities among its diverse groups.

I find it ironic that the multiracial child is still so invisible well into the 1990s. Our nation's system of racially categorizing multiracial children monoracially legitimizes their invisibility. It is the ultimate "multicultural omission," it is sanctioned by all other monoracial groups, it happens over and over again, and it could go on for decades. The fact that it has already gone on for so long is a whole research topic in itself. When I think of all the racial polarization our nation has suffered through history, shifting from one "rationalization" to another about how to define children of multiracial descent, the reasons for this state of affairs begin to become clear to me.

Racially mixed children, as distinct from monoracial children, are invisible because they fall through the cracks of our nation's attempts to keep the races "pure" even though there is no such thing as purity. In fact, the only thing pure about the races is that they are "pure fiction." Who is responsible? Do we blame the parents for marrying across color lines and not following the rules? If so, what rules have remained constant? Is it the fault of the major White cultures or that of the smaller non-White groups? It was the fault of all of us, and for this we can be united.

Perhaps we thought we were "doing the right thing," as do the politically correct of every century. Consider our previous multicultural transitions:

- We used to think it best (and some still do) to "let us say, 'they're white' if they can pass, for life will be easier for them."

- We used to think (and many still do), "Let us say, 'they're Black or Asian,' only because society will see them as such."

- We used to think, "They're Black . . . let them be loyal to *their* race," as if it were only one.

Such sociopolitical controls had the potential of silencing their inner voices. And, if anyone crossing those fixed borders even thinks about having a multiple identity, the notion that "mixed means messed" surfaces if only because multiracial students are not included. We have been a nation obsessed with our racial divisions; our racial categorization process testifies to that fact.

Until recently, identifying as "multiracial" has never been an option in this country. Now seems the time when America will begin to acknowledge and even celebrate the multiracial child. In fact, the word "multiracial" is becoming politically correct too, almost replacing "interracial." Even though most interracial families do not welcome an additional racial category, they view it as a necessary but temporary solution, while America's own racial identity is still in transition. I believe that most interracial families do not care about categories, per se, but they may believe that they are necessary in order for them to be acknowledged. "It is necessary because it will serve to—in a striking manner—get the attention of those individuals who can only view life in monolithic, monoracial terms" (Byrd 1993: 3).

The advent of a new "multiracial" category will signify the inclusion of mixed raced individuals, if only in a very technical way in the beginning. The racial categorization of mixed race children needs to be reviewed at the federal level before the public can validate the multiracial child's unique experience. Then very slowly this new way of sorting people out racially (by not sorting them out in a permeable way) will affect not only our institutional forms, our language, and our material culture, but also eventually our very idea of culture. New racial categorization will forge wider acceptance of multiple identities for interracial children and for our populace, thus enabling mixed race people to feel more comfortable with a number of identities interacting simultaneously. "Culture and history are full of borders but they are all to some degree permeable" (Hughes 1993: 95).

"Verbal uplift is not the revolution," however. A shifting of names will not alter how everyone perceives interracial children racially, nor is it meant to (Ehrenreich 1991: 336). The

American public needs to challenge the classic norms of race as being singular and fixed. And while a new "multiracial" category will have the advantage of making racially mixed children particularly visible (by highlighting their notions of difference from monoracial peoples) to the outside world, it creates a problem because such differences are not absolute to them alone. Race is a sociopolitical rather than biological construct, and even monoracial peoples need to explore possibilities for acknowledging their own "wider selves." "Rapidly increasing global interdependence has made it more and more clear that neither 'we' nor 'they' are neatly bounded and homogeneous as once seemed to be the case" (Rosaldo 1993: 217).

Writer Robert Hughes once said that "if multiculturalism is learning to see through borders, I'm in favor of it" (1993: 96). I agree, but so far I have seen very little acknowledgment—that has any real meaning—of those children who cross racial borders. For example, my daughter is applying to college and I noticed on most applications that there now seems to be some attempt to allow students to check off more than "one box" or "other" for their racial identity. However, she still receives a number of letters from colleges seeking Asian students as part of their minority recruitment programs. My review of two public school systems suggests that interracial students still count only as monoracial minorities even when there are these additional changes. Thus, while such changes may be symbolic of greater awareness of interracial children, they may actually serve to camouflage the classic norms for racially categorizing interracial students. My daughter may feel multiracial theoretically, yet she most likely will be considered to be Asian. We still do not know how she "fits in," but we feel that we have the right to know.

Racial categorization implemented in the schools and institutionalized by federal mandates is the template for how the school community (teachers, administrators, students, parents) and interracial students see themselves racially. The perceptions of the interracial child are not just tied to those particular situations that can be observed and identified in formal categorizations. They extend beyond the particular context in which the situation is framed into the real practices and everyday events of both "in school" and "out of school" culture. Thus, the schools, as one institution capable of transmitting messages (often even without knowing that they do) of both affirmation and negation for the interracial child, must take a holistic approach toward educating them.

My interviews with teachers, notation of school documents, and investigation of other aspects of both the official and hidden curricula (i.e., school cultural programs, rituals, class discussions, books, resources, and materials) indicates that the invisibility of the interracial child in the schools is wholly integrated into our wider American culture, which does not acknowledge interracial children. Yet, teachers are generally well meaning, and believe in multiculturalism. All of the teachers interviewed for this study were conscientious and sincere in their concern for their interracial students. But multiculturalism has hardly acknowledged the interracial child, and teachers may be unaware of the difficulties this invisibility may cause some interracial students.

We must redefine our concept of culture by meeting the educational needs of interracial children. Giroux argues for a "border pedagogy":

> Within this discourse, students engage knowledge as border-crossers; as people moving in and out of borders constructed around coordinates of difference and power. These are not only physical borders, but cultural borders historically constructed and socially organized within maps of rules and regulations that serve to either limit or enable particular identities, individual capacities, and social forms. Students cross borders of meaning, maps of knowledge, social relations, and values that are increasingly being negotiated and rewritten as the codes and regulations that organize them become destabilized and reshaped. Border pedagogy decenters as it remaps. (1993: 136)

It also might be helpful to some interracial students to honor those who have struggled with their identities rather than having them feel "mixed is messed." According to writer Gloria Anzaldua, "The new mestiza (persons of mixed ancestry) copes by developing a tolerance for ambiguity. . . . She learns to juggle cultures. She has a plural personality, she operates in a pluralistic mode. . . . Not only does she sustain contradictions, she turns ambivalence into something else" (1987: 79).

The interracial child with all his or her racial border crossings is a symbol of an expanding American cultural identity. We should regard such children as creative resources for developing new forms of polyglot cultural creativity. As Rosaldo says of Anzaldua, "In rejecting the classic 'authenticity' of cultural purity, she seeks out the many stranded possibilities of the borderlands. By sorting through and weaving together its overlapping strands, Anzaldua's identity becomes ever stronger, not diffused" (1993: 216).

Interracial families, who have been coping with incorporating the classic boundaries of their multiple racial identities, have created new culture, or rather "new multiculture." "They are 'new' because they are at the verge of recognition by the dominant white culture as distinct; and they are ancient because they have existed since the first tribes of different races and cultures first met" (*I-Pride Newsletter* 1992, July 19). Rather than the popular notion that the culture of multiracial children is a diluted version of their parent's heritage, racially mixed children inherit a culture in process of becoming "more" rather than something "less," from which our nation should look with an eye toward celebrating a wider sense of what it means to be an American. "The point of America was not to preserve old cultures, but to forge a new American culture" (Schlesinger 1992: 13).

We need to renegotiate and redefine our concept of culture in a way that all cultures, those separate and in between, are included rather than create another category. Separatism is not what multiracial peoples are all about, but in order to enhance their power over imposed monoracial destinies, they may have to preach a separatist attitude until there is full recognition for them. A distinctive cultural identity for the multiracial child for the time being seems to be necessary so that the cultural invisibility of interracial children will be addressed in all our institutions of learning with a view toward redefining our concept of culture.

But social change is slow and difficult. Our racial categorization system in the schools needs to reviewed and renegotiated. More awareness and dialogue on the multiracial child by the American public must take place. School personnel need to be made aware of the unique situation of the interracial child by including these students in multiculturalism and all the curricula it has created. We need to validate the uniqueness of the interracial child, not as an act of separatism, but as part of a nationwide racial re-identification, one that celebrates our connectedness to our diverse neighbors as part of our wider selves. By such inclusion, multiracial children will feel less isolated and the multicultural well-being of our nation will be increased.

Afterword

Before this book was printed, the federal Office of Management and Budget recommended the abolition of our nation's "check one box only" policy of racial statistical reporting in favor of allowing respondents to "check one or more boxes." This new standard will be used on the 2000 census and will be mandatory in our schools by 2003, ending a procedure that has made multiracial individuals invisible for over two decades. It will affect how over 2 million multiracial children report their race on school forms and how their numbers will be tallied for the federal government.

Is this a great victory for the multiracial community, which will herald the twenty-first century as a new age for multiracial individuals? Or will this alteration become a tool for masking our nation's persistence in treating multiracial individuals as monoracial? In allowing more flexibility for expressing multiracial heritage, our government also rejected another request to affirm a separate multiracial category for mixed race individuals. Therefore, our racial categorization system still leaves multiracial students without a specific identity when answering "What race are you?" on school forms.

Multiracial students' need for a cohesive multiple identity is not being met in the schools. The schools unknowingly transmit monoracial minority messages to multiracial children. Teachers and other school personnel should realize that this categorization policy is a reflection of a wider array of everyday situations that still exist in the schools. Will this alteration be sufficient to unlock how we have habitually perceived and limited racial identity possibilities for multiracial students?

Validating a multiracial category would have had a very powerful influence on public perception. A distinct multiracial category would have made racially mixed children particularly visible and empowered the multiracial community to move faster toward full inclusion of their children in the schools. It would have symbolized a national recognition of the multiracial experience and empowered its community to accomplish the tasks necessary to change the sociocultural experiences of multiracial students.

Based on our nation's past history, I am not hopeful that affirmation of multiracial identity will be offered any time soon. Multiracial children who have been denegrated in society deserve more assistance in correcting the damage that such policies have created for them. The abolition of our monoracial policy is a great victory if multiracial students are to be perceived and educated as multiracial. Unless the multiracial community calls for a renegotiation of how they are served in the schools, our nation's historical memory will continue to influence racial statistical reporting in the schools. Thus, our nation's monoracial legacy will still endure in the minds of the American public and exert its influence on how multiracial students perceive their racial identity.

Appendix A
School Forms

APPENDIX A.1:
School Registration Form

Public Schools

Name and Address of School (s) Last Attended by Child

Public _____ Private _____

Grade	School	Address	City/Town	State	Zip Code	Dates Attended
Grade	School	Address	City/Town	State	Zip Code	Dates Attended

Indicate Important Information we should know about the child - special needs or concerns:

Are there any health condition (s) which we should be aware of at school?

Allergies _____ Diabetes _____ Seizures _____ Fainting Spells _____ Medication _____ Other(s) _____

OPTIONAL SECTION

Under state law we must report the racial enrollment and native language of students at each school to assure that students are not denied any rights or benefits. If you choose, you may identify your child according to the following categories or if you do not chose to do so, we will use our best judgment. Regardless, please note that by State and Federal law no student record is available to person (s) outside the school without parental consent or a court order.

Please circle which one category best represents your child's race:

01 American Indian 03 Black, Non-Hispanic   05 Hispanic, White

02 Asian   04 Hispanic, Non-White   06 White, Non-Hispanic

What language (s) are spoken and/or understood by people living in your home?

1. English   4. Italian   7. Hebrew   10. Vietnamese

2. Spanish   5. Korean   8. Farsi   11. Other-Please Specify

3. Chinese   6. Russian   9. Greek

_____

What was the first language your child spoke? _____

_____   _____
Signature of parent or Guardian   Date

APPENDIX A.2:
Individual School Report

	GRADE	ENROLLMENT					
		1. AMERICAN INDIAN	2. BLACK (Not of Hispanic Origin	3. ASIAN	4. HISPANIC	6. WHITE (Not of Hispanic origin)	7. TOTAL
01	Pre-Kindergarten						
02	Kindergarten						
03	Ungraded						
04	Grade 1						
05	Grade 2						
06	Grade 3						
07	Grade 4						

08	Grade 5						
09	Grade 6						
10	Grade 7						
11	Grade 8						
12	Grade 9						
13	Grade 10						
14	Grade 11						
15	Grade 12						
16	Grade 13						
17	Grade 14						
18	TOTAL						

		AMER. IND PUPILS	PCT	BLACK (NOT HISP) PUPILS	PCT	ASIAN PUPILS	PCT
002000	ACTON			14	.6	134	6.2
009000	ANDOVER	6	.1	54	1.0	326	6.0
010000	ARLINGTON	1		216	5.3	228	5.6
014000	ASHLAND			46	2.4	33	1.7
017000	AUBURN	2	.1	23	1.0	17	.7
018000	AVON			75	9.4	6	.7
023000	BEDFORD	3	.2	80	4.3	81	4.3
026000	BELMONT	1		138	4.1	194	5.7
030000	BEVERLY	4	.1	111	2.3	42	.9
031000	BILLERICA	4	.1	42	.7	125	2.1
040000	BRAINTREE	3	.1	114	2.4	127	2.7
046000	BROOKLINE	6	.1	617	10.2	843	14.0
048000	BURLINGTON	1		61	1.8	226	6.6
050000	CANTON			116	4.2	58	2.1
056000	CHELMSFORD			26	.5	227	4.2
067000	CONCORD			115	6.1	62	3.3
071000	DANVERS	1		24	.7	46	1.3
073000	DEDHAM	13	.4	63	2.1	54	1.8
087000	EAST LONGMEADOW			65	2.5	12	.5
099000	FOXBOROUGH			62	2.2	40	1.4
100000	FRAMINGHAM	10	.1	657	8.8	375	5.0
101000	FRANKLIN	1		30	.7	58	1.3
110000	GRAFTON			20	1.0	41	2.1
133000	HOLBROOK	3	.2	53	3.9	17	1.3
141000	HUDSON	1		19	.7	36	1.4
155000	LEXINGTON	12	.2	370	7.0	654	12.4
158000	LITTLETON	2	.2	7	.5	22	1.7
168000	MARBLEHEAD			82	3.1	22	.8
170000	MARLBOROUGH	16	.4	125	3.0	91	2.2
178000	MELROSE	4	.1	110	3.1	54	1.5
184000	MIDDLETON			3	.5	4	.7
189000	MILTON			494	13.2	96	2.6
198000	NATICK	2	.1	114	2.9	133	3.4
199000	NEEDHAM			182	4.5	147	3.6
207000	NEWTON	6	.1	911	8.5	641	6.0
211000	NORTH ANDOVER	4	.1	35	.9	132	3.4
213000	NORTHBOROUGH	5	.3	8	.4	106	5.9
220000	NORWOOD			160	4.4	131	3.6
229000	PEABODY	6	.1	56	.9	107	1.7
244000	RANDOLPH	13	.3	902	22.6	454	11.4
246000	READING	2	.1	98	2.5	67	1.7
262000	SAUGUS	5	.2	24	.7	42	1.3
271000	SHREWSBURY	3	.1	75	1.9	213	5.5
273000	SOMERSET	6	.2	9	.3	10	.3
278000	SOUTH HADLEY			27	1.1	39	1.6

| | | | TOTAL |
| HISPANIC | | TOT MINORITY | WHITE (NOT HISP) | |
PUPILS	PCT	PUPILS	PCT	PUPILS	PCT	PUPILS	PCT
36	1.7	184	8.5	1975	91.5	2159	100.0
121	2.2	507	9.3	4954	90.7	5461	100.0
119	2.9	564	13.9	3495	86.1	4059	100.0
90	4.7	169	8.8	1757	91.2	1926	100.0
16	.7	58	2.5	2275	97.5	2333	100.0
13	1.6	94	11.7	708	88.3	802	100.0
23	1.2	187	10.0	1684	90.0	1871	100.0
37	1.1	370	10.9	3027	89.1	3397	100.0
116	2.4	273	5.7	4538	94.3	4811	100.0
75	1.2	246	4.1	5793	95.9	6039	100.0
52	1.1	296	6.3	4440	93.8	4736	100.0
261	4.3	1727	28.6	4312	71.4	6039	100.0
22	.6	310	9.1	3103	90.9	3413	100.0
22	.8	196	7.2	2537	92.8	2733	100.0
30	.6	283	5.3	5095	94.7	5378	100.0
18	1.0	195	10.4	1678	89.6	1873	100.0
31	.9	102	2.9	3433	97.1	3535	100.0
68	2.3	198	6.7	2772	93.3	2970	100.0
14	.5	91	3.5	2493	96.5	2584	100.0
34	1.2	136	4.9	2648	95.1	2784	100.0
1176	15.7	2218	29.6	5286	70.4	7504	100.0
18	.4	107	2.4	4291	97.6	4398	100.0
17	.9	78	4.0	1889	96.0	1967	100.0
37	2.7	110	8.1	1247	91.9	1357	100.0
51	2.0	107	4.2	2428	95.8	2535	100.0
59	1.1	1095	20.8	4179	79.2	5274	100.0
8	.6	39	3.1	1238	96.9	1277	100.0
20	.7	124	4.6	2560	95.4	2684	100.0
306	7.3	538	12.9	3631	87.1	4169	100.0
33	.9	201	5.6	3393	94.4	3594	100.0
6	1.0	13	2.2	569	97.8	582	100.0
37	1.0	627	16.8	3109	83.2	3736	100.0
49	1.3	298	7.6	3600	92.4	3898	100.0
62	1.5	391	9.6	3696	90.4	4087	100.0
256	2.4	1814	17.0	8866	83.0	10680	100.0
94	2.4	265	6.8	3609	93.2	3874	100.0
13	.7	132	7.4	1656	92.6	1788	100.0
104	2.8	395	10.7	3283	89.3	3678	100.0
330	5.3	499	8.1	5677	91.9	6176	100.0
225	5.6	1594	40.0	2391	60.0	3985	100.0
17	.4	184	4.6	3804	95.4	3988	100.0
15	.5	86	2.6	3193	97.4	3279	100.0
100	2.6	391	10.1	3497	89.9	3888	100.0
16	.6	41	1.4	2853	98.6	2894	100.0
39	1.6	105	4.4	2283	95.6	2388	100.0

APPENDIX A.4:
Standardized Tests

AGENCY; Executive Office of the President, Office of Management and Budget (OMB), Office of Information and Regulatory Affairs

ACTION: Notice of decision.

SUMMARY; By this Notice, OMB is announcing its decision concerning the revision of Statistical Policy Directive 15, Race and Ethnic Standards for Federal Statistics and Administrative reporting. OMB is accepting the recommendations of the Interagency Committee for the Review of the Racial and Ethnic Standards with the **following two modifications: (1) the Asian or Pacific Islander category will be separated into two categories—"Asian" and "Native Hawaiian or Other Pacific Islander," and (2) the term "Hispanic" will be changed to "Hispanic or Latino."**

The revised standards will have five minimum categories for data on race:

American Indian or Alaska Native,
Asian,
Black or African American,
Native Hawaiian or Other Pacific Islander and
White.

There will be two categories for data on ethnicity: "Hispanic or Latino" and "Not Hispanic or Latino."

Revisions to the Standards for the Classification of Federal Data on Race and Ethnicity

The OMB decisions on the Intragency Committee's specific recommendations are presented below:

(1) OMB accepts the following recommendations concerning reporting more than one race:

When self-identification is used, a method for reporting more than one race should be adopted.

The method for respondents to report more than one race should take the form of multiple responses to a single question and not a "multiracial category."

When a list of races is provided to respondents, the list should not contain a "multiracial" category.

Based on research conducted so far, two recommended forms for the instruction accompanying the multiple response question are **"Mark one or more..." and "Select one or more..."**

If the criteria for data quality and confidentiality are met, provision should be made to report, at a minimum, the number of individuals identifying with more than one race. Data producers are encouraged to provide greater detail about the distribution of multiple responses.

The new standards will be used in the decennial census, and other data producers should conform as soon as possible, but not later than January 1, 2003.

Source: Federal Register, Office of Management and Budget/October 30, 1997. Emphasis added.

APPENDIX A.5:
Attendance Reports

School Daily Count Form

Teacher _____   Room _____   Date _____

	(1) Am. Ind.	(2) Black	(3) Asian	(4) Hispanic	(5) White
Boys belonging					
Girls belonging					
Total belonging					

School Daily Count Form

Teacher _____   Room _____   Date _____

122

School Daily Count Form

Boys belonging _____
Girls belonging _____
Total belonging _____

(1) Am. Ind.	(2) Black	(3) Asian	(4) Hispanic	(5) White

Teacher _____ Room _____ Date _____

Boys belonging _____
Girls belonging _____
Total belonging _____

(1) Am. Ind.	(2) Black	(3) Asian	(4) Hispanic	(5) White

Appendix B
Federal Documents

RACE AND ETHNIC STANDARDS FOR FEDERAL STATISTICS
AND ADMINISTRATIVE REPORTING

This Directive provides standard classification for recordkeeping, collection, and presentation of data on race and ethnicity in Federal program administrative reporting and statistical activities. These classifications should not be interpreted as being scientific or anthropological in nature, nor should they be viewed as determinants of eligibility for participation in any Federal program. They have been developed in response to needs expressed by both the executive branch and the Congress to provide for the collection and use of compatible, nonduplicated, exchangeable racial and ethnic data by Federal agencies.

1. Definitions

The basic racial and ethnic categories for federal statistics and program administrative reporting are defined as follows:

a. *American Indian or Alaskan Native.* A person having origins in any of the original peoples of North America, and who maintains cultural identification through tribal affiliation or community recognition.

b. *Asian or Pacific Islander.* A person having origins in any of the original peoples of the Far East, Southeast Asia, the Indian subcontinent, or the Pacific Islands. This area includes, for example, China, India, Japan, Korea, the Philippine Islands, and Samoa.

c. *Black.* A person having origins in any of the black racial groups of Africa.

d. *Hispanic.* A person of Mexican, Puerto Rican, Cuban, Central or South American or other Spanish culture or origin, regardless of race.

e. *White.* A person having origins in any of the original peoples of Europe, North Africa, or the Middle East.

2. Utilization for Recordkeeping and Reporting

To provide flexibility, it is preferable to collect data on race and ethnic categories separately. If separate race and ethnic categories are used, the minimum designations are:

a. Race:

--American Indian or Alaskan Native

--Asian or Pacific Islander

-- Black

--White

b. Ethnicity:

--Hispanic origin

--Not of Hispanic origin

When race and ethnicity are collected separately, the number of White and Black persons who are Hispanic must be identifiable, and capable of being reported in that category.

If a combined format is used to collect racial and ethnic data, the minimum acceptable categories are:

American Indian or Alaskan Native

Asian or Pacific Islander

Black, not of Hispanic origin

Hispanic

White, not of Hispanic origin.

The category which most closely reflects the individual's recognition in his community should be used for purposes of reporting on persons who are of mixed racial and/or ethnic origins. (emphasis added)

In no case should the provisions of this Directive be construed to limit the collection of data to the categories described above. However, any reporting required which uses more detail shall be organized in such a way that the additional categories can be aggregated into these basic racial/ethnic categories.

The minimum standard collection categories shall be utilized for reporting as follows:

a. *Civil rights compliance reporting.* The categories specified above will be used by all agencies in either the separate or combined format for civil rights compliance reporting and equal employment reporting for the other public and private sectors and for all levels of government. Any variation requiring less detailed data or data which cannot be aggregated into the basic categories will have to be specifically approved by the Office of Federal Statistical Policy and Standards for executive agencies. More detailed reporting which can be aggregated to the basic categories may be used at the agencies' discretion.

b. *General program administrative and grant reporting.* Whenever an agency subject to this Directive issues new or revised administrative reporting or recordkeeping requirements which include racial or ethnic data, the agency will use the race/ethnic categories described above. A variance can be specifically requested from the Office of Federal Statistical Policy and Standards, but such a variance will be granted only if the agency can demonstrate that it is not reasonable for the primary reporter to determine the racial or ethnic background in terms of the specified categories, and that such determination is not critical to the administration of the program in question, or if the specific program is directed to only one or a limited number of races/ethnic groups, e.g., Indian tribal activities.

c. *Statistical reporting.* The categories described in this Directive will be used at a minimum for federally sponsored statistical data collection where race and/or ethnicity is required, except when: the collection involves a sample of such size that the data on the smaller categories would be unreliable, or when the collection effort focuses on a specific racial or ethnic group. A repetitive survey shall be deemed to have an adequate sample size if the racial and ethnic data can be reliably aggregated on a biennial basis. Any other variation will have to be specifically authorized by OMB through the reports clearance process (see OMB Circular No. A-40). In those cases where the data collection is not subject to the reports clearance process, a direct request for a variance should be made by OFSPS.

128

3. Effective Date

The provisions of this Directive are effective immediately for all new and revised recordkeeping or reporting requirements containing racial and/or ethnic information. All existing recordkeeping or reporting requirements shall be made consistent with this Directive at the time they are submitted for extension, or not later than January 1, 1980.

4. Presentation of Race/Ethnic Data

Displays of racial and ethnic compliance and statistical data will use the category designations listed above. The designation "nonwhite" is not acceptable for use in the presentation of Federal Government data. It is not to be used in any publication of compliance or statistical data or in the text of any compliance or statistical report.

In cases where the above designations are considered inappropriate for presentation of statistical data on particular programs or for particular regional areas, the sponsoring agency may use:

(1) The designations "Black and Other Races" or "All Other Races" as collective descriptions of minority races when the most summary distinction between the majority and minority races is appropriate;

(2) The designations "White," "Black," and "All Other Races" when the distinction among the majority race, the principal minority race, and other races is appropriate; or

3) The designation of a particular minority race or races, and the inclusion of "Whites" with "All Other Races," if such a collective description is appropriate.

In displaying detailed information which represents a combination of race and ethnicity, the description of the data being displayed must clearly indicate that both bases of classification are being used.

When the primary focus of a statistical report is on two or more specific identifiable groups in the population, one or more of which is racial or ethnic, it is acceptable to display data for each of the particular groups separately and to describe data relating to the remainder of the population by an appropriate collection description.

Note 1. Directive No. 15 supersedes section 7(h) and Exhibit F of OMB Circular No. A-46 dated May 3, 1974, and as revised May 12, 1977.

APPENDIX B.2:
Standards for the Classification of Federal Data on Race and Ethnicity

Table 1. Summary of Options for Identification of Multiracial Persons

(e) (1) Multiracial identification not allowed (must pick one broad category)

(aa) Individual chooses the one with which he or she most closely identifies

(bb) Mother's category is designated

(cc) Father's category is designated

(dd) Race of minority-designated parent (if one is White)

(e) (2) Multiracial identification allowed:

(aa) "Multiracial" category-self-identification (SI) or observer identification (OI)

(bb) "Mark all that apply: form list of specific categories-SI only

(cc) Open-ended question-SI or OI

(dd) "Other"-SI only

(ee) Mother's and father's geographic ancestry -SI only

(ff) Skin-color gradient chart-SI or OI

Pros to Option (e) (2) (aa)–"Multiracial" category:

Collection if specific races are not identified:

--Physical space on forms: adds one racial category

--Meets demand of some multiracial respondents, especially those whose parents are of different races.

--Telephone survey: Easy to ask if it is the only category added, however, if additional categories are added may be problematic.

--Somewhat more amenable to identification by observation than any other option for multiracial persons (however, compared with observation identification in Option (e)(1), this option is likely to result in an undercount and a substantially different distribution of current broad categories).

Tabulation and analysis:

--A few States passed laws to include this category in their administrative records. Currently they proportion their multiracial counts among the OMB categories for Federal reporting purposes based on percentages of minorities in the general population, although it is not clear what geographic level they are using (National, State, local, school districts, etc.) when they refer to "general population." A change in OMB to a "multiracial" category would reduce costs for these few States because they would not have to maintain data in two different ways.

--Indication of population diversity.

--Potentially useful in analyzing trends such as education and employment, especially if specific categories are identified.

Source: Federal Register/Vol. 60, No. 166/Monday, August 28, 1995/Notices

APPENDIX B.3:
Revisions to the Standards for the Classification of Federal Data on Race and Ethnicity, October 30, 1997

Massachusetts
Basic Skills
Testing
Program

GRADE 3
1990-91

STUDENT NAME:

SCHOOL NAME:

SCHOOL DISTRICT:

MARKING INSTRUCTIONS

- Use only a number 2 pencil.
- Do **NOT** use ink or ballpoint pen.
- Make heavy black marks that completely fill the circle.
- Erase completely any marks you wish to change.
- Make **NO** stray marks in this booklet.

CORRECT
○ ● ○ ○

INCORRECT
⊘ ○ ⊗ ○○

BACKGROUND INFORMATION
(SEE ADMINISTRATOR'S MANUAL FOR INSTRUCTIONS)

1. YOU ARE:

   ○ MALE ○ FEMALE

2. YOU ARE:

   ○ BLACK (not Hispanic) ○ HISPANIC

   ○ WHITE (not Hispanic) ○ OTHER

   ○ ASIAN

PROGRAM INFORMATION
(SEE ADMINISTRATOR'S MANUAL FOR INSTRUCTIONS)

CURRENTLY IN SPECIAL EDUCATION?

○ YES ○ NO

IF YES, WHICH PROTOTYPE?

○ 502.1 ○ 502.3

○ 502.2 ○ 502.4

CURRENTLY IN BILINGUAL PROGRAM?

○ YES ○ NO

132

LANGUAGE PROFICIENCY

○ FLUENT ENGLISH
○ LIMITED ENGLISH
○ NON-ENGLISH SPEAKING

PARENT REPORT

○ SPANISH
○ PORTUGUESE

STUDENT EXEMPTED FROM:

○ READING TEST
○ MATHEMATICS TEST
○ WRITING TEST

---

3. **HOW OFTEN DO PEOPLE IN YOUR HOME SPEAK A LANGUAGE OTHER THAN ENGLISH?**

○ NEVER   ○ MOST OF THE TIME
○ SOMETIMES   ○ ALWAYS
○ ABOUT HALF THE TIME

4. **ABOUT HOW MANY BOOKS OF YOUR OWN, NOT COUNTING YOUR SCHOOL BOOKS OR COMIC BOOKS, DO YOU HAVE AT HOME?**

○ 5 OR FEWER   ○ 16 - 30
○ 6 - 15   ○ MORE THAN 30

5. **DID YOU GO TO ANY SCHOOL BEFORE YOU STARTED KINDERGARTEN?**

○ YES   ○ NO   ○ I DON'T KNOW

133

Appendix C

Checklist of School Services for Multiracial Students

Parents need to insure their children's inclusion in all school curriculum and classroom practices by asking questions such as the following:

1. Do all teachers understand their students' multiracial heritage and do they affirm it for them as they do for students of other ethnic/racial groups?

2. When race is a topic in books, cultural programs, class discussions, conferences and other aspects of the formal curriculum, do teachers include multiracial students as a distinct group?

3. Does your school have books and other resources and materials about multiracial children?

4. Do history books provide multiracial students with information on significant multiracial individuals?

5. Will multiracial students be able to easily access information about themselves from their libraries?

Further Reading

BOOKS FOR MULTIRACIAL CHILDREN

Early Childhood

Adoff, Arnold. 1973. *Black Is Brown Is Tan*. New York: Harper Row.
Davol, Marguerite W. 1993. *Black, White, Just Right!* Morton Grove, Ill.: Whitman Publishing.
Mandelbaum, Phil. 1990. *You Be Me / I'll Be You*. Brooklyn, N.Y.: Kane Mill Book Publishers.
Nye, Loyal. 1977. *What Color Am I?* Nashville: Abingdon.
Williams, Garth. 1958. *The Rabbits' Wedding*. New York: Harper.
Williams, Vera. 1990. *More More More Said the Baby*. New York: Greenwillow Books.

School Age

Adoff, Arnold. 1982. *All the Colors of the Race*. New York: Lothrop.
———. 1991. *Hard to Be Six*. New York: Lothrop.
Angel, Ann. 1988. *Real for Sure Sister*. Fort Wayne, Ind.: Perspectives Press.
Blume, Judy. 1970. *Are You There God? It's Me Margaret*. New York: Dell Publishing.

Friedman, Ina R. 1984. *How My Parents Learned To Eat*. Boston: Houghton Mifflin.

Gridley, Marion. 1973. *Maria Tallchief*. Minnesota: Dillon Press.

Igus, Toyomi. 1996. *Two Many Mrs. Gibsons*. San Francisco: Children's Book Press.

Lacapa, Kathleen, and Michael Lacapa. 1994. *Less Than Half, More Than Whole*. Flagstone, Ariz.: Northland Publishing.

Mansch, Robert. *Something Good*. 1996. Toronto: Annick Press Limited.

Miles, Betty. 1976. *All It Takes Is Practice*. New York: Knopf.

Ringgold, Faith. 1996. *Bonjour Lonnie*. New York: Hyperion Books.

Rosenberg, Maxine. *Living in Two Worlds*. New York: Lothop, Lee & Shepard Books.

Sanders, Doris. 1990. *Clover*. Carrboro, N.C.: Algonquin Books of Chapel Hill.

Tate, Eleanora B. 1985. *Just an Overnight Guest*. New York: Dial Press.

Young Adult

Danziger, Paula. 1985. *It's an Aardvark Eat Turtle World*. New York: Delacorte Press.

Garland, Sherry. 1992. *Song of the Buffalo Boy*. New York: Harcourt Brace Jovanovich.

Hamilton, Virginia. 1974. *M. C. Higgins, The Great*. New York: Collier Books.

———. 1976. *Arilla Sun Down*. New York: Dell Publishing.

Kandel, Bethany. 1997. *Trevor's Story: Growing Up Biracial*. Minneapolis: Lerner Publications.

Little, Mimi Otey. 1996. *Yoshiko and the Foreigner*. New York: Farrar, Strauss and Giroux.

Lipsyte, Robert. 1991. *The Brave*. New York: HarperCollins.

Meyer, Carolyn. 1997. *Jubilee Journey*. New York: Harcourt Brace and Company.

Pullman, Phillip. 1992. *The Broken Bridge*. New York: Harcourt Brace Jovanovich.

Roy, Jacqueline. 1992. *Soul Daddy*. New York: Harcourt Brace Jovanovich.

Taylor, Mildred D. 1981. *Let the Circle Be Unbroken*. New York: Bantam Books.

Woodson, Jacqueline. 1997. *The House You Pass on the Way*. New York: Delacorte Press.

Wyeth, Sharon Dennis. 1994. *The World of Daughter McGuire*. New York: Delacorte Press.

———. 1995. *Ginger Brown: Too Many Houses*. New York: Random House.

———1997. *Ginger Brown: The Nobody Boy*. New York: Random House.

Bibliography

Anzaldua, Gloria. 1987. *Borderlands La Frontera: The New Mestiza*. San Francisco: Spinsters/Aunt Lute.

Apple, Michael. 1993. *Official Knowledge: Democratic Education in a Conservative Age*. New York: Routledge.

Arnold, M. C. 1984. "The Effects of Racial Identity on Self-Concept in Interracial Children." Ph.D. diss., Saint Louis University.

Atkinson, Paul. 1990. *The Ethnographic Imagination*. London and New York: Routledge.

Barron, M. L. 1972. *The Blending American: Patterns of Intermarriage*. Chicago: Quadrangle Books.

Bennet, Christine. 1986. *Comprehensive Multicultural Education*. Boston: Allyn and Bacon.

Benson, S. 1981. *Ambiguous Ethnicity*. New York: Cambridge University Press.

Berman, Paul, ed. 1992. *Debating P.C.: The Controversy Over Political Correctness on College Campuses*. New York: Dell.

Bernard, Jessie. 1966. "Note on Educational Homogamy in Negro White and White Negro Marriages." *Journal of Marriage and Family* 27: 274–276.

Bossard, J. 1939. "Nationality and Nativity as Factors in Marriage." *American Sociological Review* 4: 792–798.

Bradshaw, C. K. 1990. "A Japanese View of Dependency: What Can
    Amae Psychology Contribute to Feminist Theory and Therapy?"
    In *Diversity and Complexity in Feminist Therapy*, edited by L.
    Brown and Maria Root. New York: Haworth.
Brayboy, Thomas L. 1966. "Interracial Sexuality as an Expression of
    Neurotic Conflict." *Journal of Sex Research* 2, no. 3: 179–184.
Brown, John A. 1987. "Casework Contacts with Black-White Couples."
    Social Casework (January): 24–29.
Brown, Ursula M. 1995. "Black/White Interracial Young Adults: Quest
    for a Racial Identity." *American Journal of Orthopsychiatry* 65,
    no.1: 125–130.
Bureau of Data Collection of the Massachusetts Department of Edu-
    cation. October 1, 1990 and 1996.
Burma, John H. 1963. "Interethnic Marriage in Los Angeles, 1948–
    1959." *Social Forces* 42: 154–168.
Byrd, Charles. 1993. *Interracial Voice* 2, no. 4: 3.
Char, W. F. 1977. "Motivations for Intercultural Marriages." In *Ad-
    justment in Intercultural Marriages*, edited by W. S. Tseng and
    T. W. Maretzki. Honolulu: University Press of Hawaii, 33–40.
Cheng, C. K., and D. S. Yamamura. 1957. "Interracial Marriage and
    Divorce in Hawaii." *Social Forces* 36 (October): 77–84.
———. 1984. "Children of Interracial Families." *Interracial Books for
    Children* 15, no. 6.
Connor, John W. 1976. *A Study of the Marital Stability of Japanese
    War Brides*. San Fransisco: R & E Research Associates.
Cooley, Charles Horton. 1964. *Human Nature and the Social Order*.
    New York: Schocken.
Corrigan, Phillip. 1989. "Playing . . . Contradictions, Empowerment
    and Empowerment: Punk, Pedagogy, and Popular Cultural
    Forms (On Ethnography and Education)." In *Popular Culture
    Schooling and Everyday Life*, edited by Henry Giroux and Roger
    Simon. Westport, Conn.: Bergin & Garvey.
Cotter, J. S. 1990. "The Mulatto to His Critics." *Complete Poems*. Re-
    print. Athens: University of Georgia Press.
Crester, Gary, and Joseph Leon. 1982. "Intermarriage in the U.S.: An
    Overview of Theory and Research." *Journal of Marriage and
    Family Review* 5: 3–15.
De Leo, Robert. 1997. Massachusetts House Bill No. 2259.
De Vos, George, and Horoshi Wagatsuma. 1972. *Japan's Invisible
    Race*. Berkeley.
Douglas, Mary. 1986. *How Institutions Think*. Syracuse: Syracuse Uni-
    versity Press.

Durkheim, Emile, and M. Mauss. 1903. "De Quelques Formes Primitives de la Classification: Contribution à L'Étude des Representations Collectives." *L'Année Sociologique* 6: 1–72.

Edwards, Melvin. 1989. "The Classification Issue: Let's Continue to Be Heard." *The Communique Newsletter*. Houston: Interracial Family Alliance.

Ehrenreich, Barbara. 1991. "The Challenge for the Left." In *Democratic Left* XIX (July/August), no. 4.

Epps, Edgar. [1929] 1974. *Cultural Pluralism*. Reprint. Berkeley: McCutchan Publishing.

Erikson, E. H. 1963. *Childhood and Society*. New York: Norton Press.

———. 1966. "The Concept of Identity in Race Relations: Notes and Queries." *Daedalus* 95: 145–177.

Fanon, Franz. 1967. *Black Skin, White Masks*. New York: Grove Press.

Faulkner, Jan. 1985. "Women in Interracial Relationships." *Women and Therapy* 2, nos. 2–3: 191–203.

Faulkner, Jan, and G. K. Kich. 1983. "Assessment and Engagement Stages in Therapy with the Interracial Family." *Family Therapy Collections* 6: 78–90.

Fernandez, Carlos. 1989. *The Communique Newsletter*. Issue 2. Houston: Interracial Family Alliance.

———. 1996. *The Multiracial Experience*, edited by Maria Root. Newbury Park, Calif.: Sage.

Fleck, Ludwik. 1935. *The Genesis and Development of a Scientific Fact*. Chicago: University of Chicago Press.

Foucault, Michel. 1970. *The Order of Things: An Archaeology of Human Sciences*. New York: Pantheon Books.

Freire, Paulo, and Ira Shor. 1987. *A Pedagogy for Liberation: Dialogues on Transforming Education*. Westport, Conn.: Bergin & Garvey.

Fullerton, Gail. 1977. *Survival in Marriage*. Hinsdale: Dryden Press.

Gibbs, Jewelle Taylor. 1987. "Identity and Marginality: Issues in the Treatment of Biracial Adolescents." *American Journal of Orthopsychiatry* 57, no. 2: 265–278.

Giroux, Henry A. 1983. *Theory and Resistance in Education*. Westport, Conn.: Bergin & Garvey.

———. 1988. *Teachers as Intellectuals: Toward a Pedagogy of Learning*. Westport, Conn.: Bergin & Garvey.

———. 1993. *Border Crossings: Culture Workers and the Politics of Education*. Westport, Conn.: Bergin & Garvey.

Giroux, Henry A. and Roger Simon. 1989. *Popular Culture: Schooling and Everyday Life*. Westport, Conn.: Bergin & Garvey.

Gordon, A. I. 1964. *Intermarriage*. Boston: Beacon Press.

Gordon, M. 1964. *Assimilation in American Life*. New York: Oxford University Press.

Goffman, Erving. 1984. *Stigma*. Englewood Cliffs, N.J.: Prentice Hall.

Hall, C. C. 1980. "The Ethnic Identity of Racially Mixed People: A Study of Black/Japanese." Ph.D. diss., Los Angeles: University of California.

———. 1992. "Please Choose One: Ethnic Identity Choices for Biracial Individuals." In *Racially Mixed People in America*, edited by Maria P. Root. Newbury Park, Calif: Sage, 250–264.

Hall, Edward T. 1959. *The Silent Language*. Garden City, NY: Doubleday.

Heer, David. 1966. "Negro-White Marriage in the United States." *Journal of Marriage and Family* 27: 262–273.

Henriques, F. 1974. *Children of Caliban*. London: Secker and Warburg.

Hollis, D. 1991. "A Legacy of Loving." *New People* 2: 9–12.

Hughes, Robert. 1993. *Culture of Complaint*. Oxford and New York: Oxford University Press.

Hutnik, Nimmi. 1986. "Patterns of Ethnic Minority Identification and Modes of Social Adaptation." *Ethnic and Racial Studies* 9, no. 2: 150–167.

Interracial Voice. January 29, 1966.

I-Pride Newsletter. July 19, 1992.

Jacobs, H. 1977. "Black/White Interracial Families: Marital Process and Identity Development in Young Children." Ph.D. diss., Honolulu: University of Hawaii at Manoa.

Jeter, Kris. 1982. "Analytic Essay: Intercultural and Interracial Marriage." *Marriage and Family Review* 5: 101–111.

Johnson, R., and C. Nagoshi. 1986. "The Adjustment of Offspring of Within-Group and Interracial/Intercultural Marriages: A Comparison of Personality Factor Scores." *Journal of Marriage and Family* 48: 279–284.

Kich, G. K. 1982. "Ethnic, Racial Identity Development of Biracial Japanese/White Adults." Ph.D. diss. Berkeley, Calif.: Wright Institute.

———. 1992. "The Developmental Process of Asserting Biracial, Bicultural Identity." In *Racially Mixed People in America*, edited by Maria P. Root. Newbury Park, Calif.: Sage, 304–317.

King, Laurie, ed. 1994. *Hear My Voice*. New York: Addison Wesley.

Kitano, H. L., and Lynn Chai. 1981. "Korean Interracial Marriage." *Marriage and Family Review* 5: 75–89.

Kitano, H. L., and Wai-Tsang Yeung. 1982. "Chinese Interracial Marriage." *Marriage and Family Review* 5: 35–48.

Kitano, H. L., Wai-Tsang Yeung, L. Chai, and H. Hatanaka. 1984. "Asian American Interracial Marriage." *Journal of Marriage and Family* 46: 179–190.

Lieberman, L., Blaine W. Stevenson, and Larry Reynolds. 1989. "Race and Anthropology." *Anthropology and Education Quarterly* 20: 67–72.

Lincoln, Bruce. 1989. *Discourse and Construction of Society.* Oxford: Oxford University Press.

Lyles, M. R., A. Yancey, C. Grace, and J. H. Carter. 1985. "Racial Identity and Self-Esteem: Problems Peculiar to Biracial Children." *Journal of the American Academy of Child and Adolescent Psychiatry* 24: 150–153.

Mar, J. 1988. "Chinese Caucasian Interracial Parenting and Ethnic Identity." Ph.D. diss., Amherst: University of Massachusetts.

Marcia, J. 1980. "Identity in Adolescence." *Handbook of Adolescent Psychology.* New York: John Wiley.

McLaren, Peter. 1986. *Schooling as a Ritual Performance.* Boston: Routledge and Kegan Paul.

———. 1989. *Life in Schools: An Introduction to Critical Pedagogy in the Foundations of Education.* White Plains, N.Y.: Longman.

McRoy, R., and E. Freeman. 1986. "Racial Identity Issues among Mixed Race Children." *Social Work in Education* 8, no. 3: 164–174.

Monahan, T. P. 1973. "Marriage across Racial Lines in Indiana." *Journal of Marriage and Family* 35: 632–640.

Murguia, R., and E. Cazares. 1982. "Intermarriage of Mexican Americans." *Marriage and Family Review* 5: 91–99.

Murphy-Shigematsu, S. L. 1986. "The Voices of Amerasians: Ethnicity, Identity and Empowerment in Interracial Japanese Americans." Ph.D. diss., Cambridge: Harvard University.

Nakashima, Cynthia. 1992. "An Invisible Monster: The Creation and Denial of Mixed Race People in America." In *Racially Mixed People in America*, edited by Maria P. Root. Newbury Park, Calif.: Sage.

Njeri, I. 1988. "A Sense of Identity." *Los Angeles Times.* June 5.

Park, R. E. 1928. "Human Migration and the Marginal Man." *American Journal of Sociology* 33: 881–893.

Porterfield, E. 1978. *Black and White Mixed Marriages.* Chicago: Newson Hall.

Poussaint, A. 1975. "The Problems of Light Skinned Blacks." *Ebony* 30: 85–88.

———. 1984. "Study of Interracial Children Presents Positive Picture." *Interracial Books for Children* 15, no. 6: 9–10.

Root, Maria P., ed. 1992. *Racially Mixed People in America*. Newbury Park, Calif.: Sage.

———. 1996. *The Multiracial Experience*. Newbury Park, Calif.: Sage.

Rosaldo, Renato. 1989. *Culture and Truth*. Boston: Beacon Press.

Rose, Nikolas. 1989. "Individualizing Psychology." *In Texts of Identity*. Newbury Park, Calif.: Sage.

Schlesinger, Arthur M., Jr. 1992. *The Disuniting of America*, New York: W. W. Norton.

Shackford, K. 1984. "Interracial Children: Growing Up Healthy in an Unhealthy Society." *Interracial Books for Children* 15, no.6: 4–6.

Slugoski, B. R., and G. P. Ginsburg. 1989. "Ego Identity and Explanatory Speech." In *Texts of Identity*, edited by J. Shotter and K. Gergen. Newbury Park, Calif.: Sage.

Sommers, Vita S. 1964. "The Impact of Dual-Cultural Membership on Identity." *Psychiatry* 27: 332–344.

Spickard, Paul. 1989. *Mixed Blood: Intermarriage and Ethnic Identity in Twentieth Century America*. Madison: University of Wisconsin Press.

Spindler, George D. 1967. "The Transmission of Culture." *Culture in Process*, edited by Alan Beals. New York: Holt, Rhinehart and Winston.

Spivey, Philip. 1984. "Interracial Adolescence: Self Image, Racial Self Concept and Family Process." Ph.D. diss., New York: City College.

Statistical Policy Directive 15. 1978. Race and Ethnic Standards for Federal Statistics and Administrative Reporting. Office of Management and Budget.

Stonequist, E. V. 1937. *The Marginal Man*. New York: Russell and Russell.

Taylor, Charles. 1994. *Multiculturalism*. Princeton, N.J.: Princeton University Press.

Teicher, J. 1968. "Some Observations on Identity Problems in Children of Negro-White Marriage." *Journal of Nervous and Mental Disorders* 146: 249–256.

Tinker, J. 1982. "Intermarriage and Assimilation in a Plural Society: Japanese Americans in the United States." *Marriage and Family Review* 5: 61–74.

U.S. Department of Education. National Center for Education Statistics. 1996. *Racial and Ethnic Classifications Used by Public Schools*, NCES 96–92, by Nancy Carey and Elizabeth Farris. Judi Carpenter, project officer. Washington D.C.

Wallman, S. 1983. "Identity Options." *Minorities: Community and Idenity*, edited by C. Fried. New York: Springer Verlag.

Wardle, F. 1988. "Growing Up Biracially in America: The Inalienable Rights of Biracial Children." *Nurturing Today* (winter): 9–21.

―――. 1989. "Culture and Biracial Children: A Conflict or Alliance?" *The Communique*, issue 2. Houston: Interracial Family Alliance.

―――. 1991. "Interracial Children and Their Families: How School Social Workers Should Respond." *Social Work in Education* 13: 209–272.

Waters, Mary C. 1990. *Ethnic Options: Choosing Identities in America.* Berkeley: University of California Press.

Wilden, A. 1980. *System and Structure: Essays in Communication and Exchange.* London: Tavistock.

Wilkinson, D. 1975. *Black Male/White Female.* Cambridge: Schenkman Publishing.

Willet, Gerri. 1993. Notation from author's Ph.D. thesis advisor, University of Massachussetts, Amherst.

Williams, Teresa Kay. 1992. "Prism Lives: Identity of Binational Amerasians." *Racially Mixed People in America*, edited by Maria Root. Newbury Park, Calif.: Sage.

Williamson, Joel. 1984. *The New People: Miscegenation and Mulattoes in the United States.* New York: New York University Press.

Wilson, A. 1987. *Mixed Race Children: A Study of Identity.* London and Boston: Allen and University Press.

Young, Iris Marion. 1990. *Justice and the Politics of Difference.* Princeton, N.J.: Princeton University Press.

Index

About the Author

JANE AYERS CHIONG was Founder and Director of Boston's first non-profit agency for interracial families, The Multiracial Family Network. She has also taught for many years in colleges and community agencies, and is currently owner and Director of The Math and Reading Centers.

ISBN 0-89789-499-5

9 780897 894999

90000>

EAN

HARDCOVER BAR CODE